FENCING
ESSENTIAL SKILLS TRAINING

ED ROGERS

CROWOOD

First published in 2003 by
The Crowood Press Ltd
Ramsbury, Marlborough
Wiltshire SN8 2HR

www.crowood.com

British Library Cataloguing-in-Publication Data
A catalogue record for this book is available from the British
Library.

ISBN 1 86126 594 8

Dedication
This book is dedicated to my lovely wife Hilary.

Acknowledgements
With special thanks to Mike Fitchett, Lorraine Rose, Neil
Melville, Bob Jamieson, Graham Morrison, Vladimir Fonov,
Bert Bracewell and the members of Heriot-Watt University
Fencing Club.

The photographs on pages 2, 9, 93, 101, 161, 167 and 221 are
courtesy of Graham Morrison; those on pages 20, 21 and 24 are
courtesy of Vladimir Fonov; and that on page 169 (below) is
courtesy of Bert Bracewell. All the other photographs were
taken with permission at Heriot-Watt University Fencing Club.
Drawings are by the author.

Designed and typeset by Focus Publishing, Sevenoaks, Kent
Printed and bound in Great Britain by
Bookcraft, Midsomer Norton

Contents

Introduction 6

Part One: Foil 9

1 Foil Training 10

2 Advanced Foil Training 42

3 Coaching Foil 94

Part Two: Sabre 101

4 Sabre Training 102

5 Advanced Sabre Training 125

6 Coaching Sabre 162

Part Three: Épée 167

7 Épée Training 168

8 Advanced Épée Training 190

9 Coaching Épée 222

Glossary 227

Bibliography 233

Index 235

Introduction

The *Mary Rose* sank in 1545. At that time, a book on archery was published in which the author complained of neglect in that sport in favour of fencing, which had masters in every town. The man behind this was Henry VIII, who encouraged displays of swordplay and who had in 1540 given the London Masters of Defence a monopoly of teaching arms. Henry clearly understood the importance of skills training in fencing, which is the art and science of handling the sword. The fundamental elements of fencing skills are timing, speed and distance. Controlling distance between yourself and your opponent is at the centre.

Fencing flourished during the Renaissance. For duel and combat purposes, much training concentrated on thrusts to the torso where hits would have the most lethal effect. This led to the development of safe training weapons, protective clothing and limited valid target areas. The foil was used for practice, with a button placed on the point for safety. Its target area was limited to the torso, which could be easily padded. To avoid potentially dangerous simultaneous attacks, the right of way was given to the person first initiating the attack. These rules were intended to simulate real combat and have been incorporated into the modern sport.

To become an Olympic fencer requires years of dedicated training. Mastering skills in a logical and progressive manner is an essential prerequisite to efficient performance. The time taken to develop these skills will vary depending on the individual. Each new skill should be combined with previously learned skills. Observation of experienced fencers will add meaning to these skills. All fencing actions must be mastered at all distances and with a variety of footwork combinations. More advanced fencers may also vary their timing. Each weapon has its own unique cadence. When learning a new action or combination of actions, first execute it perfectly at slow speed, then the speed can be gradually increased.

Fencing mobilizes the individual's muscles, intellectual powers and emotional energies. Training tests the fencer's willpower, patience and perseverance, by the repeated performance of technical exercises over extended periods of time. This requires self-discipline, concentration and co-ordination, combined with controlling the emotions. Tactical training tends to follow technical training. Actual combat (bout fencing) only comes after a thorough preliminary training and prolonged practice. Qualities such as detachment, balance, quick thinking, precise observation, sense of distance, the ability to recognize the opponent's intentions, foresight, the ability to execute complex movements, timing and so on emerge after several years of training.

Certain actions are common to the foil, sabre and épée and all require a high degree of co-ordination. Initially, the learning process may be split up into stages for learning purposes. Try not to do this in a disjointed way – work slowly but maintain the rhythm. Lastly, try to picture the entire action as it would be perfectly executed, then do it. The distance between yourself and your opponent is important. Two right-handed (or two left-handed) fencers will fence/train at a set distance, depending on the weapon. A right- and left-handed combination is different in that these fencers will find their nearest target areas approximately 150mm closer and some compensation in distance is necessary to allow for this.

The on-guard position is the 'get ready' position for the fencer. To be on guard is to be prepared to execute defensive actions when attacked, or to launch an offensive action when the opportunity arises. Whether training or participating in a bout, a fencer needs to be mentally alert from the start. A good on-guard position combined with neat footwork will allow you to change direction at a moment's notice, with central balance. Remember to keep your body upright and your weight evenly distributed on both feet. Your knees should always point in the same direction as your feet.

People who train regularly should use a training plastron, which is a padded over-jacket, so as to avoid discomfort from repetitive hits. My first plastron was homemade and cost very little to make. A protective sleeve is also essential when practising repetitive hits at épée or cuts to the wrist and arm at sabre. Similarly, leg or foot protection is required when practising repetitive hits to leg or foot at épée.

Always work at a speed at which you feel comfortable. Start as slow as you like, then gradually speed up while concentrating on technique. It is advisable to train using as small an action as possible, because in a real fighting situation these actions will get bigger. Train at 100 per cent effort, because when fencing competitively you are likely to fence at 70 per cent, in order to save something for later on. Fencers who train together will agree at the outset signals that can be used to initiate any given training sequence. These might involve the presentation of the blade, a verbal signal, or perhaps a signal given with the unarmed hand.

The age at which young people start fencing training varies throughout the world; some start as early as eight years old. For young fencers, training should be portrayed more as a game, rather than as a learning experience. It is important to emphasize safety with young people – their technique will follow. When choosing a fencing club always ask what organized training is available. While group footwork training will develop mobility, individual lessons with a coach will improve technical skills and increase knowledge. Fencers who elect to compete on a regular basis should plan their training to fit their competitive programme. Get to know your coaches well.

Whilst there are a number of excellent books on fencing available, I feel there is a niche for a book that can help fencers to train in a club situation. The best way to learn about fencing is being taught by a professional coach, but regular lessons may not always be possible. Working from this book should help fencers to supplement their training.

Treat this volume as a workbook. While it contains a representative sample of many traditional fencing actions, it is not meant to be an all-embracing reference work. The notation used refers to Fencer A and Fencer B and is written from the point of view of two right-handed fencers (or two left-handed fencers). Where additional comments are required to adapt for a left- and right-handed combination, these have been added. Spend about 50 per cent of your time as Fencer A, then swap over. Fencer A always initiates the play. Coaches wishing to use this workbook as an aid to coaching should always take the part of Fencer A and adopt the teaching position instead of standing on guard. Feel free to adapt any of these sessions to suit your own interests and change the order if you think this makes more sense for you. Add your own favourites.

Many fencers who regularly train never aspire to Olympic heights, yet choose to attend clubs and compete in regional and national events where they can fence as an individual or as part of a team. Some find fencing simply a good form of exercise. This is one of the few physical activities in which men and women can take part and train on equal terms. It is also a good sport if (like me) you wear glasses, as once the fencing mask is on you can just forget about them. Veteran fencing (fencing for the over-forties) is on the increase, even for people who have never fenced before.

Always warm up your muscles before you train or fence. First get your blood pumping through them by doing some form of exercise, which should include stretching exercises. Now you are ready to do a warm-up routine with a friend. Try to devise a routine that you like and which lasts about four to five minutes. Move progressively from simple to more complex actions, leading slowly from immobility to concentrated (intense) activity and then back to immobility again. Offensive and defensive movements can be alternated if you need to catch your breath.

Like any student of fencing, I openly acknowledge the influences of all the masters and experienced fencers that I have trained with, but in particular those of my own fencing master, Professor H T Bracewell.

PART ONE
Foil

CHAPTER ONE

Foil Training

Introduction

The foil is the modern version of the original practice weapon for the duelling sword. The valid target at this weapon is the body torso. The foil has a flexible rectangular blade. Valid hits are scored with the point and are hits that arrive correctly on target. Fencers wear metallic jackets, which allow hits to be registered by an electronic scoring apparatus. If a fencer hits directly on to the metallic jacket, a coloured light registers that the hit has landed. If the hit lands on the legs or arms (off-target), a white light is registered. A hit off-target stops the fencing phrase. If you hit the floor, an off-target light comes on, unless you are fencing on a copper piste, which is the linear strip on which the fencing bout is fought.

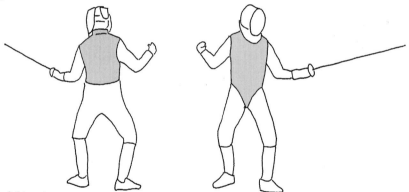

The foil target.

A beginner might start with a foil training weapon that has a relatively flexible blade with a plastic button on the end. An electric foil, which many experienced fencers choose to train with, has a metal tip which depresses on contact with the metallic jacket when fencing in a bout, so as to record the hit. Training and repetitively hitting the same spot using an electric foil can cause discomfort, hence the need to use a plastron.

The foil is a conventional weapon. The first person to attack has right of way, and there are defined rules of engagement. The referee plays an important role by deciding who receives the scored hit.

On-guard and footwork

The on-guard position in foil aims to ensure balance and mobility. The feet are a normal walking pace apart and at right angles, with the heels in line. The centre of gravity of the body is central between the feet. The elbow of the sword arm should be about the width of a hand away from the hip. The foil is held to one side so that the fencer is covered (a defensive position where the fencer cannot be hit on that side), and the point is usually about mouth level. The rear hand is held high. To be on guard is to be equally prepared to carry out defensive or offensive actions. It is the ready position adopted before the word 'play' which starts a bout. Foilists fence toe to toe (opposing front feet in line). Originally it was front toe to opponent's back toe.

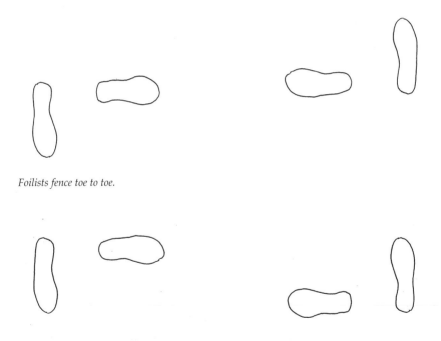

Foilists fence toe to toe.

Originally it was front toe to opponent's back toe.

Fencing measure is the distance at which one can hit the opponent's target with a lunge. A lunge is an attack made by extending the rear leg and landing on the bent front leg. At foil, to hit the valid target requires a hit to the torso, hence fencing measure is lunging distance to torso.

To lunge, start by extending the sword arm three-fifths of the way and begin to lift the toes on the front foot. On the straightening of the arm immediately lunge.

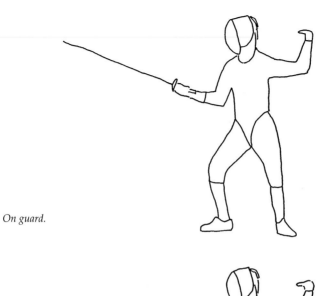

On guard.

Extend the sword arm three-fifths of the way and begin to lift the front foot.

On the straightening of the arm immediately lunge.

   In this position, the front knee should be over the instep, the rear leg locks, with the rear foot flat on the ground with toes slightly turned forward. The rear hand goes back, with the palm facing upward to assist balance.

The lunge position.

The recovery is the return to the on-guard position, by moving forward or backward. In this case, we will recover to guard by moving backward. First, bend the back leg to return to guard without lifting the body. Pull the back arm up to return, leaving the sword arm straight until the front heel has landed. Lastly, bend the sword arm. The return to guard is as important as the lunge. A forward recovery is called a reprise. Here the rear arm is used as a counterbalance, which is lifted up in time with the rear leg moving forward.

Return to guard.

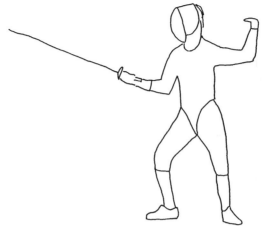

On guard.

To step forward, move the front foot forward heel–toe, followed by the rear foot toe–heel. To step backward, move the rear foot backward toe–heel, followed by the front foot heel–toe. At this stage, try to keep your steps all the same size.

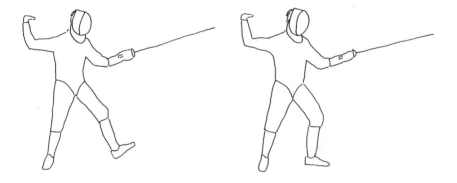

Move the front foot forward heel–toe ...   *... followed by the rear foot toe–heel.*

Retreating with a crossover can be effective against a rapidly advancing opponent. Advancing with a crossover is potentially dangerous. To move backward with a crossover, place the front foot behind the rear foot, then the rear foot backward (keeping both feet at right angles to each other), returning to the on-guard position.

A balestra is a small jump forward, which precedes an attack. The front foot sharply strikes the floor and the on-guard position which follows may be a little crouched.

The flèche extends the attacker's reach a little further than a lunge. Start by fully extending the sword arm, allowing the head and body to move forward. The body's centre of gravity moves forward, causing a toppling action. The fencer pushes off assertively with the front foot (without the head rising), driving the attack horizontally forward (not upward), bringing the rear leg forward with a crossover action in order to recover balance. Try to hit before the rear leg levels the ground.

Start by fully extending the sword arm.

Bring the rear leg forward in order to recover balance.

The flèche is a fully committed action and should not be used too often, as any action fully committed can be potentially dangerous. Avoid a large step with the rear leg action, as this can reduce momentum. Finish by running past and around the opponent, without physical contact. Another way of transferring the weight forward is to move the front foot backward with the straightening of the sword arm.

A flèche can also be performed from a lunge. Start from a short lunge position:

- lean forward a little, pushing with the rear toe and bringing up the rear arm, to get as much weight forward as possible, then push off with the front foot
- or, bring the front foot back a little, bringing up the rear arm to transfer weight forward, then push off with the front foot
- or, bring the rear foot forward (three-quarters recovery only), then bring the front foot back as before, and so on. The short action of the rear foot gets weight moving forward as quickly as possible.

Whilst many of the training exercises which follow will be executed from a position where the blades are engaged (in contact), much of modern foil is carried out with absence of blade (blades not in contact).

There are nine guards at foil (and épée), which are as follows:

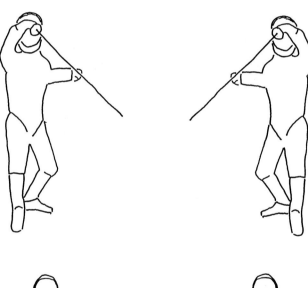

Prime.

Seconde.

Tierce.

Quarte.

Quinte.

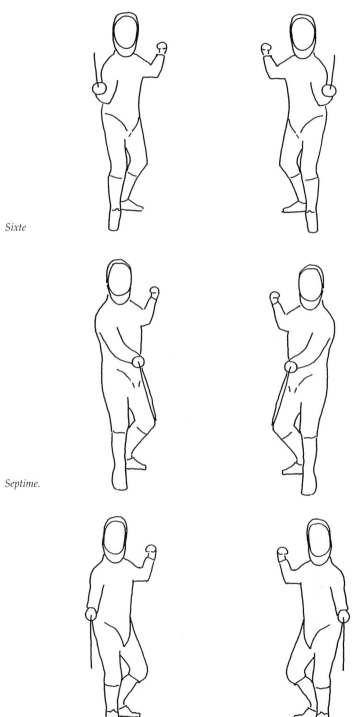

Sixte

Septime.

Octave.

Raised sixte.

The ninth was taught to me under the term 'raised sixte', but others may know this as 'neuvieme'.

Control of the Weapon

Weapons are available for right- or left-handed fencers. Foil handles are usually either of French-design or are orthopaedic (also called a pistol grip), which is moulded to fit the hand.

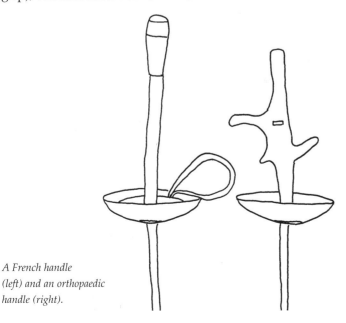

A French handle (left) and an orthopaedic handle (right).

A French-designed handle is shaped to fit the hand. Place the first phalanx of your index finger under the handle close to the guard (coquille), the thumb resting flat on top of the handle. The remaining three fingers rest along the side of the handle. The handle lies centrally on the palm. When on guard, there should be a straight line between the elbow and the point.

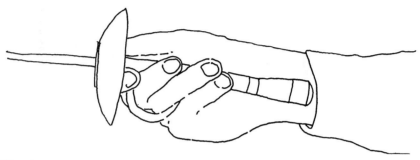

The grip.

Learning to grip the foil correctly.

From the on-guard position, straighten the sword arm and place the point of the sword on the opponent's body. Rotate the index finger and thumb so that the point hits with the character of penetration, with a biting action.

Start at straight arm distance to body. The blades are engaged with the centre of the blades in contact.

Placing the hit.

Fencer A

1   In sixte.
Slowly turns hand a little toward quarte.

Lightly taps the centre of the blade as a signal.
• This action is to make the fencer cover on return to guard. So many fencers are lazy in this respect. One must always remember that an action is not complete until a fencer has returned to a covered defensive position.

Fencer B

In sixte.
Straightens the sword arm in response to the opening line and (neatly) hits with point to chest (just bending the blade).

Bends sword arm and resumes on-guard position in sixte.

(Left-handed/right-handed combination: Fencer B is covered with opponent's blade engaged on the outside. Fencer A turns hand a little toward sixte.)

Fencer A now varies the timing, trying to ensure that the actions of the hand are as small as possible.

Simple Attacks

A simple attack, direct or indirect, is correctly executed when the straight-ening of the arm, the point threatening the valid target, proceeds the ini-tiation of the lunge or the flèche. An attack is an attempt by the fencer to hit the opponent. A flèche is an attack with a crossover action of the feet and can typically be used when the opponent has retreated to just outside lunge distance. An action is indirect if it finishes in a different line to the one in which it was formed. Simple attacks can be delivered from a posi-tion of engagement, or with absence of blade. They take the straightest route to the valid target which may be directed to the high or low lines.
   Simple attacks consist of a:

- straight thrust – a direct simple attack into the line in which the fencer is engaged
- disengagement – an indirect simple attack passing the point under the blade from the line of engagement into another line
- cutover – a type of disengagement that passes over the blade from the line of engagement into another line (also called a coupé)
- counter-disengagement – which deceives the opponent's change of engagement or counter-parry (circular).

Start at lunge distance to body with blades engaged.

Fencer A	Fencer B
1 In sixte. Steps forward and turns hand a little toward quarte.	In sixte. Straightens the sword arm in response to the opening line and hits with point to chest.
Lightly taps the blade as a sig-nal to return to guard and steps backward.	Bends sword arm and resumes the on-guard position in sixte.
2 In sixte. Turns hand a little toward quarte.	In sixte. Straightens the sword arm in

	response to the opening line, lunges and hits with point to chest as front foot lands (keeping hand approximately head height on the lunge).
Lightly taps the blade as a signal to return to guard.	First bends the back leg to start to recover to guard, then recovers to guard with the sword arm still straight. The front foot lands on the heel. Bending the sword arm is the last action.

3 In sixte.
Steps backward and turns hand a little toward quarte.

In sixte.
Straightens the sword arm in response to the opening line, steps forward and lunges with hit to chest.

Lightly taps the blade as a signal to return to guard.

Recovers as before.

4 In sixte.
Steps backward.
After the step turns the hand a little toward quarte.

In sixte.
Steps forward.
Straightens the sword arm in response to the opening line and lunges with hit to chest.

Lightly taps the blade as a signal to return to guard.

Recovers as before.

(Left-handed/right-handed combination: Fencer B is covered with opponent's blade engaged on the outside. Fencer A turns hand a little toward sixte.)

Now try a disengagement at lunge distance to body with blades engaged.

Fencer A

Fencer B

1 In sixte.
Steps forward and pressures the blade lightly in the

In sixte.
Disengages under the blade in response into the opening line,

A simple attack.

direction of sixte.
• With attacks or feints the action must be into an open or opening line.

lifting the point to the same height on the other side. Straightens the sword arm and hits with point to chest.
• The careful use of the fingers should ensure that the motion of the point is as economical as possible.

Lightly taps the blade as a signal to return to guard.

Recovers as before.

2   In sixte.
Pressures blade lightly in the direction of sixte.

In sixte.
Disengages under the blade in response to the opening line and straightens the sword arm, then lunges and hits with point to chest as front foot lands.

Lightly taps the blade as a signal to return to guard.

Recovers as before.

3   In sixte.
Pressures blade lightly in direction of sixte and steps backward.

In sixte.
Disengages under the blade in response to the opening line,

Practising disengaging and lunging with point to chest.

	straightens the sword arm and steps forward, then lunges and hits with point to chest.
Lightly taps the blade as a signal to return to guard.	Recovers as before.
4 In sixte. Steps backward. After the step, pressures the blade lightly in the direction of sixte. Lightly taps the blade as a signal to return to guard.	In sixte. Steps forward. Disengages under the blade in response to the opening line, then lunges and hits with point to chest. Recovers as before.

(Left-handed/right-handed combination: Fencer B is covered with opponent's blade engaged on the outside. Fencer A turns hand a little toward quarte.)

Try the same openings, but this time with Fencer B responding by cutover. With the cutover do not draw the hand back, but use the manipulation of the fingers to just clear the top of the opponent's blade, then straighten immediately.

Parries and Ripostes

The parry is a defensive action made with the blade to prevent the attack from landing. The principle of defence is the opposition of forte to foible. The forte is the strong part of the blade nearest the guard. The foible is the upper weak part. Parries can be:

• lateral – moving from side to side (also called a simple parry)
• circular – where the point moves in a complete circle (also called a counter-parry)
• semicircular – moving from high to low line, or from low to high line, where the point moves in a semi-circle.

To understand which type of parry is being performed, first observe the starting position, then follow the shape made by the point. If you move to sixte from quarte, the point moves in a straight line. If you are in sixte and your opponent does a disengagement, you can move around the opponent's blade with a circular action, returning to sixte. If you are in octave (the parry below sixte, which covers the low line), and your opponent attacks in the high line, you can parry sixte by making a semicircular action. In all three examples you end up in sixte, but have different starting points and travel by different routes.

Semicircular parries tend to be more like a 'U' on its side rather than a semicircle, in order to gather the blade. A circular parry of octave tends to be elliptical, rather than circular in order to protect the target on top of the shoulder above the sword arm.

The on-guard position is usually sixte (but you can also fence from other defensive positions). If you move laterally to the other side of the target area, this is quarte. Below sixte is octave. Below quarte is septime. These hand positions describe a small defensive box, within which much of the foil defence can be made. These are termed supinated (or half-supinated) parries (palm tends to be upward). There are also pronated parries (palm tends to be downward), which will be covered in Chapter 2 on Advanced Foil Training.

When stepping backward, first move the rear foot, then parry with the landing of the front foot, which allows the riposte to be made from a stable (well-balanced) position.

The riposte is the offensive action made by the fencer who has successfully parried the attack. This can be direct, indirect or compound and delivered immediately or after a delay, by detachment or with opposition.

Start at straight arm distance to body.

Fencer A	**Fencer B**
1 In sixte. Places the end of the blade alongside Fencer B's chest, lightly touching the side of the torso.	In sixte. Moves hand across to quarte so that opponent's blade is just deflected from the target. • The defender's point should be positioned to hit the opponent's target by the shortest possible route. • Do not lower the point when moving the hand from sixte to quarte. • Use as small a lateral hand action as possible. • Lastly, riposte with detachment by straightening the sword arm on the sixte side.
Steps backward.	Bends sword arm and resumes on-guard position in sixte.

(Left-handed/right-handed combination: the sixte position for Fencer B is a little further out, in the direction of sixte. The size of the parry remains the same.)

With the next exercise, both fencers should try to keep their hand actions to the bare minimum. The parries must be neat and you should be careful not to let the point drift out, because this increases the distance to be covered by the riposte.

Start at straight arm distance to body. The inside of the blade is the side of the blade in which the line is open if the fencer is on guard in sixte. The outside of the blade is the side of the blade in which the line is closed if the fencer is on guard (covered) in sixte.

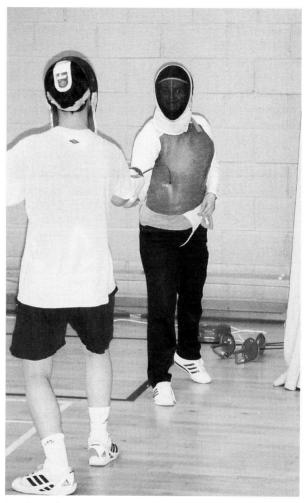

Practising placing the riposte.

Fencer A	**Fencer B**
1	Places point of the weapon on Fencer A's chest and leaves it there.
In sixte. Taps blade lightly on the inside and extends to Fencer B's quarte side.	Neatly parries quarte and ripostes back to same spot on Fencer A's chest and leaves it there.
Taps blade lightly on the out-	Neatly parries sixte and

side and extends to Fencer B's sixte side	ripostes back to same spot on Fencer A's chest and leaves it there
Taps blade lightly on the outside and extends to Fencer B's quarte side.	Neatly parries quarte and ripostes back to same spot on Fencer A's chest and leaves it there.
Taps blade lightly on the inside and extends to Fencer B's sixte side.	Neatly parries sixte and ripostes back to same spot on Fencer A's chest and leaves it there.
Steps backward.	Bends sword arm and resumes on-guard position in sixte.
2	Places point of the weapon on Fencer A's chest and leaves it there.
In sixte. Now carries out the above four actions randomly.	Neatly parries quarte or sixte appropriately in response, ripostes back to same spot on Fencer A's chest and leaves it there.
Continues to practise until ready to finish.	
Steps backward to finish.	Bends sword arm and resumes on-guard position in sixte.

To practise counter-parries, Fencer B should stand on guard in sixte or quarte. Fencer A will then lay the tip of the blade on the (top) inside of Fencer B's guard. Fencer B practises a circular action with the finger, gathering the blade on the other side.

To practise semicircular parries, Fencer B should stand on guard in sixte or quarte. Fencer A will then lay the tip of the blade in the inside five o'clock position of Fencer B's guard. Fencer B practises a semicircular 'U'-shaped action to gather the blade.

Counter-Ripostes

The counter-riposte is an offensive action made by the fencer who has successfully parried the riposte or counter-riposte. The attacker has the odd numbers with counter-ripostes, the defender the even numbers. Lengthy counter-riposte sequences are not common in the modern sport. They can be taken on the lunge, or after returning to guard. They can be reflex actions, or as the result of premeditation (second intention). A second-intention action is used to draw a response from an opponent. If parrying on the lunge, imagine you are parrying with the elbow and keep the point in line with the target.

Start at lunge distance to body with blades engaged.

First we will set up a situation where Fencer A initiates a realistic parry and riposte. Having established this successfully, Fencer B will next introduce the counter-riposte.

Fencer A	**Fencer B**
1 In sixte. Gives agreed signal for the training sequence to begin.	In sixte. When ready, pressures the blade lightly in the direction of sixte, opening the line to Fencer A's target which was previously covered.
Returns the pressure in response. • This is done in order to cover the exposed target.	Does cutover immediately and lunges into the opening line.
Parries quarte and ripostes with point to chest. Then bends sword arm and resumes on-guard position in sixte.	Recovers to guard after the hit successfully lands.
2 In sixte. Gives agreed signal for the training sequence to begin.	In sixte. When ready, pressures the blade as before.
Returns the pressure in response.	Does cutover immediately and lunges.

Parries quarte and attempts riposte with point to chest.

Immediately parries quarte on the lunge and counter-ripostes to chest.

Lightly taps the blade as a signal to return to guard.

Recovers to guard.

3 In sixte.
Gives agreed signal for the training sequence to begin.

In sixte.
When ready, pressures the blade as before.

Returns the pressure in response.

Does cutover immediately and lunges.

Parries quarte and pauses.

Recovers to guard.

Lunges with the riposte.

Parries quarte and counter-ripostes to chest.
• On returning to guard, ensure that the centre of gravity of the body is central between the feet and the point is at about mouth level.

Recovers to guard after Fencer B's hit successfully lands.

4 In sixte.
Gives agreed signal for the training sequence to begin.

In sixte.
When ready, pressures the blade as before.

Returns the pressure in response.

Does cutover immediately and lunges.

Parries quarte and attempts riposte with point to chest.

Recovers forward, parries quarte and counter-ripostes to chest

Lightly taps the blade as a signal to return to guard and steps backward.

Bends sword arm and resumes on-guard position in sixte.

(Left-handed/right-handed combination: the opponent's blade is on Fencer B's outside. Fencer B is covered. Fencer A parries sixte.)

Compound Attacks

A compound attack comprises of one or more feints. A successful feint must convince the defender that it is a real attack. All actions must resemble the real thing. A feint of an attack must start in an open or opening line. If the defender does not parry, then the simple attack should land. To a parry of quarte, the attacker might do a disengagement during the lunge while the front foot is still moving forward (this is called a progressive attack), and the hit will land on the other side of the blade when the front foot lands (or before). Be careful not to hit the sword arm after the disengagement. This type of compound attack is called a one–two. A compound attack can begin with any simple attack, followed by a second action into a different line.

In order to ensure that the hit lands cleanly, we can do some skills training at close quarters.

Fencer A	Fencer B
In sixte. Holds unarmed hand on front of chest with forefinger horizontal.	In sixte. Straightens the sword arm and lays tip of blade (the last 50mm) on the finger. Adjust distance as required.
Lightly taps blade on the inside.	Does small disengagement and places the tip of the blade back on Fencer A's finger. • This finger action is done primarily with the thumb and index finger with the other fingers assisting. • Try to keep the movement of the point as economical as possible.
Lightly taps blade on the outside	Does small disengagement as before and places the tip of the blade back on Fencer A's finger
Continues to practise until ready to finish.	
Steps backward to finish.	Bends sword arm and resumes on-guard position in sixte.

Now try the same exercise with Fencer B on a lunge.

In the next exercise both fencers start on guard in sixte at lunge distance with the blades engaged. Start with a successful disengagement attack, which will help to make the feint nice and deep. Imagine a tactical situation where the attacker has hit with a simple attack. Next time, the parry should come out quickly, so that the attacker is obliged to go compound.

Fencer A	Fencer B
1 In sixte. Gives agreed signal for the training sequence to begin.	In sixte. When ready, pressures the blade lightly in the direction of sixte.
Returns the pressure in response.	Disengages and lunges with point to chest. • Fencer A now has a reason to parry.
Lightly taps the blade as a signal to return to guard.	Recovers to guard.
2 In sixte. Gives agreed signal for the training sequence to begin.	In sixte. When ready, pressures the blade lightly in the direction of sixte.
Returns the pressure in response.	Disengages and starts to lunge with a feint to chest to draw the parry. • If Fencer A does not parry, then the attack would simply proceed directly to the target as before.
Parries quarte.	Disengages progressively during the course of the lunge and hits with point to chest. • Fencer B has had to begin to lunge in order to draw the parry. • The disengagement takes

	place while the front foot is still in motion and the point is moving continuously toward the target. • Great care must be taken to avoid hitting the off-target area around the hand.
Lightly taps the blade as a signal to return to guard.	Recovers to guard.
3 In sixte. Gives agreed signal for the training sequence to begin.	In sixte. When ready, pressures the blade lightly in the direction of sixte and takes a fast small step forward. • This places point closer to Fencer A's target.
Returns the pressure immediately in response and takes a fast small step backward.	Disengages and starts to lunge with a feint to chest to draw the parry.
Parries quarte.	Disengages progressively during the course of the lunge and hits with point to chest.
Lightly taps the blade as a signal to return to guard.	Recovers to guard.

(Left-handed/right-handed combination: the opponent's blade is on Fencer B's outside. Fencer B is covered. Fencer A parries sixte.)

This action can also finish in the low line. The hand is turned in pronation during the lunge with the blade parallel to the ground, or the point angled a little upward. The blade bends to the side, instead of perpendicularly. This type of compound attack is called a high–low.

Start at lunge distance to body with the blades engaged.

Fencer A	**Fencer B**
In sixte. Gives agreed signal for the training sequence to begin.	In sixte. When ready, pressures the blade lightly in the direcion of sixte.

Returns the pressure in response.	Disengages and starts to lunge with a feint to chest to draw the parry.
Parries quarte.	Turns the hand in pronation during the course of the lunge and lunges with point to the low line of the valid target.
Lightly taps the top of the blade as a signal to return to guard.	Recovers to guard

(Left-handed/right-handed combination: the opponent's blade is on Fencer B's outside. Fencer B is covered. Fencer A parries sixte.)

Successive Parries and Ripostes

Successive parries are a response to a compound attack. The first parry can be taken a little earlier in order to provide sufficient time for the second to be formed. The second is timed to coincide with the last action of the attack, which is into a known line. Later, a small step backward can be used in conjunction with the second parry, in order to increase its effectiveness.

Start at lunge distance to body with the blades engaged.

Fencer A	**Fencer B**
1 In sixte. Pressures the blade lightly in the direction of sixte.	In sixte. Returns the pressure in response.
Disengages and starts to lunge with a feint to chest to draw the parry.	Starts to parry quarte early. Does not move the hand all the way to quarte. • This is done to allow time for the second parry.
During the course of the lunge disengages around the blade to evade the early parry.	Parries sixte immediately and ripostes with point to chest.
Recovers to guard after Fencer B's hit successfully lands.	

2

Fencer A	Fencer B
In sixte. Pressures the blade lightly in the direction of sixte.	In sixte. Returns the pressure in response.
Disengages and starts to lunge with a feint to chest to draw the parry.	Starts to parry quarte early.
During the course of the lunge disengages around the blade to evade the early parry.	Parries counter-quarte immediately and ripostes with point to chest. • Try to ensure that the point does not drop during the counter-parry.
Recovers to guard after Fencer B's hit successfully lands.	

(Left-handed/right-handed combination: the opponent's blade is on Fencer B's outside. Fencer B is covered. Fencer A pressures the blade lightly in the direction of quarte.)

Both of these examples can now be performed with both fencers' blades engaged in quarte. This time, the responses will be sixte then quarte and sixte followed by counter-sixte.

Now we can introduce a counter-disengagement into the phrase. This is like a disengagement, but with a small circular action of the point that is achieved by using the fingers.

Start at lunge distance to body with the blades engaged.

Fencer A	**Fencer B**
In sixte. Pressures the blade lightly in the direction of sixte.	In sixte. Returns the pressure in response.
Disengages and starts to lunge with a feint to chest to draw the parry.	Starts to parry counter-sixte early.
During the course of the lunge counter-disengages around the blade to evade the early parry.	Parries quarte immediately and ripostes with point to chest.

Recovers to guard after Fencer
B's hit successfully lands.

(Left-handed/right-handed combination: the opponent's blade is on
Fencer B's outside. Fencer B is covered. Fencer A pressures the blade lightly in the direction of quarte.)

Preparations

A preparation of attack is any action that prepares the way. Such actions
can be made with the feet, the blade, or both.

Typical movements of the feet:

- step – step forward or backward, with or without crossover
- appel – a blow on the ground made with the ball of the foot as a preparation and to distract the opponent
- balestra – a jump forward, followed by some more footwork (like a
  lunge).

Typical blade actions:
- pressure – pressing against an opponent's blade, in order to deflect it, or
  to get a reaction
- beat – a striking action on the opponent's blade (either of the lateral
  sides plus top and underside of the blade)
- croisé – carrying the opponent's blade from high to low line, or low to
  high line on the same side as the engagement
- bind – when the blades are engaged, carrying the opponent's blade
  diagonally across from high to low line, or low to high line
- envelopment – where the weak part of the opposing blade is taken by
  the strong part of the attacker's blade, describing a circle, with both
  blades in contact, returning to the same line of engagement
- coulé – starts by gliding along the adverse blade, keeping it in opposition, raising the hand at the last minute to create a sudden opposition of
  forte to foible
- engagement – when the blades are in contact
- change of engagement – passing from one engagement to another by
  moving under the blade
- change beat – a beat executed with a change of engagement
- froissement – displaces the opponent's blade by a strong grazing action.

To execute a change of engagement, start at lunge distance to body with
the blades engaged.

Fencer A	**Fencer B**
1 In sixte. Gives agreed signal for the training sequence to begin.	In sixte. When ready, changes engagement from sixte to quarte by moving under the blade. Fencer A is now vulnerable on the quarte side of the target. Lunges with point to chest.
Lightly taps the blade as a signal to return to guard.	Recovers to guard

(Left-handed/right-handed combination: the opponent's blade is on Fencer B's outside. Fencer B is covered. Fencer A is vulnerable on the sixte side of the target.)

Fencer A	**Fencer B**
2 In sixte. Gives agreed signal for the training sequence to begin.	In sixte. When ready, changes engagement from sixte to quarte, then starts to lunge.
Parries quarte, reacting.	Disengages progressively during the course of the lunge and hits with point to chest. • This is a one–two compound attack preceded by a blade preparation.
Lightly taps the blade as a signal to return to guard.	Recovers to guard
3 In sixte. Gives agreed signal for the training sequence to begin.	In sixte. When ready, takes a small step forward and changes engagement from sixte to quarte then starts to lunge. • The small step forward puts Fencer B's point closer to the opponent's target.
Parries quarte more quickly, with a fast, small step backward (reacting).	Disengages progressively during the course of the lunge and hits with point to chest.

Lightly taps the blade as a sig-   Recovers to guard.
nal to return to guard.

(Left-handed/right-handed combination for 2. and 3.: the opponent's
blade is on Fencer B's outside. Fencer B is covered. Fencer A parries sixte.)

Now try the previous sequence using a high–low compound attack.
   Here, we try some footwork preparations with absence of blade, at step
and lunge distance to body.

Fencer A	**Fencer B**
1 In sixte. Gives agreed signal for the training sequence to begin.	In octave. Steps forward, then straightens the sword arm and lunges with hit to chest.
Lightly taps the blade as a signal to return to guard.	Recovers to guard.
2 In sixte. Gives agreed signal for the training sequence to begin.	In octave. Does balestra, then straightens the sword arm and lunges with hit to chest. • With the balestra both feet move at the same time, which makes it faster than a step.
Lightly taps the blade as a signal to return to guard.	Recovers to guard.

Attacks on the Preparation

This can be any attack launched into any preparation. Typically, it is an
attack with a lunge launched into the opponent's advance.
   Start at step and lunge distance to body.

Fencer A	**Fencer B**
1 In sixte.	In sixte.
Steps forward as a preparation to attack.	Lunges into the preparation before Fencer A's attack

• Fencer A is now within lunge distance to body.	develops and hits to chest.
Lightly taps the blade as a signal to return to guard.	Recovers to guard.

Next, Fencer B gets the opponent to step forward by first stepping backward, thus increasing the distance between them.

This time start at lunge distance to body with blades engaged.

2	In sixte. Gives agreed signal for the training sequence to begin.	In sixte. Steps backward. • The distance between the two fencers is now step and lunge distance to body.
	Fencer A is too far away to hit the opponent's target with a lunge, so steps forward to close the distance between them. • Fencer A has committed to moving forward and is now vulnerable.	Begins lunge into the preparation in response to Fencer A's front foot moving forward. Hits to chest as the step is completed. • On completion of the step the distance between the two fencers is lunge distance to body.
	Lightly taps the blade as a signal to return to guard.	Recovers to guard.

(Left-handed/right-handed combination: the opponent's blade is on Fencer B's outside. Fencer B is covered.)

Fencer A has been hit on the preparation. Next time Fencer B attacks, Fencer A applies second intention and attempts to parry and riposte. Second intention is where a premeditated action is used to draw a response from the opponent, which prepares the way for the intended action that follows. Fencer B does not take the bait, but responds with a compound attack into the opponent's preparation.

Start at lunge distance to body with blades engaged.

3	In sixte. Gives agreed signal for the training sequence to begin.	In sixte. Steps backward. • The distance between the two fencers is now step and lunge distance to body.

Steps forward to close the distance.	Starts to lunge into the preparation.
Fencer A anticipates the line into which Fencer B may attack and intends to draw the hit in order to parry and riposte.	
Parries quarte. Fencer A was hit the last time, so this time reacts quickly.	Disengages progressively during the course of the lunge and hits with point to chest.
Lightly taps the blade as a signal to return to guard.	Recovers to guard.

(Left-handed/right-handed combination: the opponent's blade is on Fencer B's outside. Fencer B is covered.)

If Fencer A takes a slightly larger step, then the fencers will end up a little closer together. If fencer B takes a slightly larger step then they will end up a little further apart. The intention when training is that the blades are lightly bent when the hit lands and that the point hits with the character of penetration, just enough to register a hit. In general when training, if you find that you are too close to an opponent when carrying out an action, make adjustment to suit.

Next, Fencer A attempts a blade preparation.

Start at lunge distance to body with blades engaged.

Fencer A	**Fencer B**
In sixte. Changes engagement from sixte to quarte.	In sixte. Counter-disengages and lunges with hit to chest. • This should be done with a neat finger action. • Ensure that the arm is straight before the front foot moves forward.
Lightly taps the blade as a signal to return to guard.	Recovers to guard.

(Left-handed/right-handed combination: the opponent's blade is on Fencer B's outside. Fencer A's line is open and responds by moving under the blade and attempting to cover in sixte.)

CHAPTER TWO

Advanced Foil Training

Introduction

Point control is essential in foil. Touching the arm, leg or mask inadvertently with the point invalidates any hit that follows. Accuracy is achieved by repeating actions again and again and always attempting to hit the same spot. If you carry out an action one hundred times and you hit successfully eighty times, then you are 80 per cent efficient. Efficiency of point control is most important in a fencing competition, where the final seeding for the competition can begin with the scores from the first bout.

Simple attacks

The use of simple attacks is common at advanced level. Good timing and footwork are essential, as well as the ability to change direction flawlessly, without leaning forward or backward. One of the best times to launch any attack is when your opponent is stepping forward.

Start with Fencer B coming on guard in sixte. Fencer A does not have a weapon, but instead, with the gloved hand, attempts to touch Fencer B's blade. Both fencers are wearing masks. The object of the game is to avoid the touch. Fencer B evades these actions and when an opportunity presents itself launches a simple attack. If there is no response, this might be a straight thrust; to a quarte type movement of the hand, a disengagement; or to a counter-sixte type of movement of the hand, a counter-disengagement. This is called 'open eye' training, where Fencer B has to respond to Fencer A's actions, which, as in a real fencing situation, can vary.

Now Fencer A holds a weapon and the same exercise is repeated, varying the distance.

Parries and Ripostes

There are certain parries made at foil and épée that are executed in pronation. These are prime, seconde, tierce and quinte. These are particularly effective against someone attempting to force the blade through the defence with angulation, and at close quarters. Ripostes from pronated parries need considerable practice. The distance is different and so is the angle of the hit.

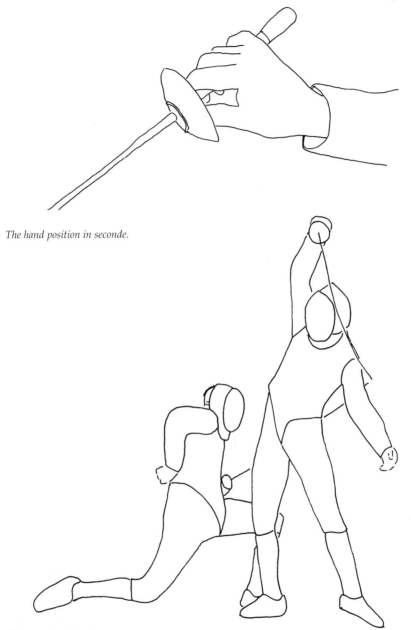

The hand position in seconde.

Close quarters fencing.

Seconde at foil is similar to the sabre parry of seconde. Rotate your forearm from sixte (keeping your hand the same height), turning the hand until the knuckles are uppermost. The grip shifts a little during the rotation of the forearm. The hand moves marginally forward, which ensures that the elbow stays behind the hand and does not stick out.

Tierce at foil and épée is similar. The sabre parry of tierce is taken lower down. Use the fingers and wrist to manipulate the weapon. Turn the hand from sixte until the knuckles are uppermost. The blade and forearm should form a straight line.

Prime is similar at all three weapons. A high prime is particularly useful at foil where the point ends up close to the valid foil target (the torso), ready for a direct riposte.

Quinte at foil and épée is similar. Here the hand is placed well forward, on the quarte side, with the knuckles turned uppermost. The sabre parry of quinte is designed to defend against a cut to head.

Start is different and at close quarters at straight arm distance to body.

Fencer A	**Fencer B**
1 In sixte. Slides blade slowly down the sixte side of the blade, looking for a slight opening at top of shoulder.	In sixte. Practises turning the hand slowly with an opposing action to tierce.
2 In sixte. Extends blade slowly on the quarte side of the blade, a little above the guard.	In sixte. Practises turning the hand slowly to seconde, with a sharp gathering action.
3 In sixte. Extends blade slowly on the quarte side of the blade, a little above the guard.	In sixte. Practises turning the hand slowly in pronation, moving it forward a little and rotating to quinte.
4 In sixte. Extends blade slowly on the quarte side of the blade, the hand a little higher.	In sixte. Practises turning the hand slowly to prime, lifting the hand high.

(Left-handed/right-handed combination: the opponent's blade is on Fencer B's outside. Fencer B is covered.)

Whilst there are many different technical variations to the parry of quarte, the following offers nine practical examples which can be practised in quick succession. Start with the traditional economic parry of quarte learned in the previous chapter.

Fencer A	**Fencer B**
1	Places point of the weapon on Fencer A's chest and leaves it there.
In sixte. Taps blade lightly on the inside. and extends to Fencer B's quarte side.	Neatly parries quarte and ripostes back to same spot on Fencer A's chest and leaves it there.
2 In sixte. Taps blade lightly on the inside and extends to Fencer B's quarte side.	Neatly parries quarte, lifting the point with the blade at 45 degrees to the horizontal, and ripostes back to same spot on Fencer A's chest and leaves it there.
3 In sixte. Taps blade lightly on the inside and extends to Fencer B's quarte side.	Neatly parries quarte, lifting the point with the blade at 80 degrees to the horizontal, and ripostes back to same spot on Fencer A's chest and leaves it there.
4 In sixte. **5** Taps blade lightly on the inside **6** and extends to Fencer B's quarte side.	Lifts the hand a little in quarte and repeats 1., 2., 3.
7 In sixte. **8** Taps blade lightly on the inside **9** and extends to Fencer B's quarte side.	Lowers the hand a little in quarte and repeats 1., 2., 3.

(Left-handed/right-handed combination: the opponent's blade is on Fencer B's outside. Fencer B is covered.)

Do all nine parries, slowly to start with, rhythmically in succession. Try always to hit the same spot. It is essential to use a plastron during this exercise, particularly if hitting regularly in the same spot using an electric foil.

Now try a different way of using some of the parries learned earlier. Start at lunge distance to body with blades engaged.

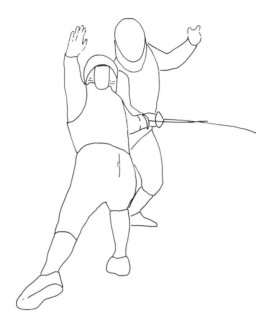

A wide parry of quarte.

Fencer A	**Fencer B**
1 In sixte. Pressures the blade lightly toward sixte.	In sixte. Disengages under the blade and does three-quarters lunge. • The point is still short of the target. • This is a probing attack. Fencer B is looking for a reaction.
Fencer A is intending to do a late parry, so does not respond.	Recovers backward to guard with the hand well forward in the middle of the target and the blade horizontal.
• A horizontal blade can be difficult to beat. Lunges with attack on either side of the blade.	Does short parries by rotating the hand to either side and ripostes with detachment. If Fencer A attacks on the sixte side, parries sixte or counter-quarte. If Fencer A attacks on the quarte side, parries quarte or counter-sixte.

(Left-handed/right-handed combination: the opponent's blade is on Fencer B's outside. Fencer B is covered. To start, Fencer A pressures the blade lightly toward quarte.)

Next, do this same exercise again, but sometimes turn the wrist suddenly (to get a sharp hand action), which will get more speed into the parry and riposte. If Fencer B's initial attack was parried, then this type of response would virtually eliminate the possibility of a compound riposte being initiated by Fencer A.

2	In sixte. Pressures the blade lightly toward sixte.	In sixte. Disengages under the blade and does three-quarters lunge.
	Fencer A does not respond.	Recovers backward to guard with the hand well forward in the middle of the target and the blade horizontal.
	Lunges with attack on either side of the blade.	Introduces short, sharp parries randomly, as well as ordinary parries, by rotating the hand to either side and ripostes with opposition. If Fencer A attacks on the sixte side, parries sixte or counter-quarte. If Fencer A attacks on the quarte side, parries quarte or counter-sixte. If Fencer A attacks to the forward top shoulder, then tierce can be used.

(Left-handed/right-handed combination: the opponent's blade is on Fencer B's outside. Fencer B is covered.)

By combining the parries and ripostes into one action, these responses can all be converted into time thrusts.

The next routine starts at lunge distance to body with absence of blade.

Fencer A	**Fencer B**
1 In sixte.	In octave.

Gives agreed signal for the training sequence to begin.	Lifts the point and attempts to engage the blade in sixte or quarte.
Deceives the blade and lunges with hit to chest. • At no point do the blades touch.	Parries quarte or sixte as required and ripostes with point to chest.

Finishing with a second intention compound riposte.

2	In sixte. Gives agreed signal for the training sequence to begin.	In octave. Lifts the point and attempts to engage the blade in sixte or quarte.
	Deceives the blade and lunges with hit to chest.	Parries quarte or sixte and feints riposte to chest. The point comes forward quickly, driving Fencer A back to guard, reacting instinctively with a lateral parry.
	Recovers to guard and takes a lateral parry.	Deceives parry and lunges with point to chest or low line. Fencer B responds to the timing of Fencer A's parry. • At no point do the blades touch.

Now Fencer B's hand moves from octave diagonally to quarte. This technique is called 'cutting the line'. Start at lunge distance to body with absence of blade.

3	In sixte. Does straight thrust from absence of blade.	In octave. Moves hand diagonally from octave to the parry of quarte and ripostes to chest.

(Left-handed/right-handed combination: parries quarte and ripostes with angulation to flank. Cutting the line is particularly useful in helping to expose the opponent's flank.)

This is a way of speeding up the riposte.

4	In sixte. Does straight thrust from	In octave. Parries quarte, as blades lightly

absence of blade.

touch deliberately applies some additional pressure to opponent's blade and ripostes immediately to chest.

Another way to speed up the riposte is by narrowing the timing of the window of opportunity available.

5   In sixte.
Does straight thrust from absence of blade.

In octave.
Parries quarte, and begins to riposte.

Attempts to deflect the point away from the target by lightly tapping the blade.
• This leaves a window of opportunity into which Fencer B has to hit successfully.
• By gradually speeding up this hand action the opportunity to hit is gradually reduced and the riposte must speed up.

• The riposte must land before the blade is knocked aside.
• Always try to hit the same spot.

Against an opponent who likes to remise try:

6   In sixte.
Does straight thrust from absence of blade.

In octave.
Parries quarte and ripostes with croisé to flank, or keeps going around and finishes with a hit to chest.

If an opponent ducks down and drops the rear shoulder in an attempt to avoid being hit, then take the hit around and place it on the target next to the rear shoulder. The croisé is performed by first parrying quarte, then the hand turns a little (but still in the same position), making the point move a further 50mm toward the quarte side. This places the defender's blade directly on top of the attacker's. Lastly, the hand drops a little and the point is placed on the target, still holding on to the blade.

(Left-handed/right-handed combination: ripostes with croisé to chest or keep going around and finishes with angulated hit to back If the opponent ducks down keeps the hand high and place the hit high on the back.)

The next routine is good for developing the fingers and the ability to deceive the blade. This is a training exercise used for developing skill, not a combat scenario. Start slowly. Master the first action, then slowly introduce the others one at a time. Build up a rhythm.

Start at lunge distance to body with the blades engaged.

Fencer A	**Fencer B**
1 In sixte. Pressures the blade lightly toward sixte.	In sixte. Disengages and starts to lunge.
Parries counter-sixte.	Does a counter-disengagement progressively during lunge and lightly hits to chest. Leaves the point on the chest and waits for Fencer A's signal.
Taps the blade on the quarte side as a signal to recover to guard.	Recovers backward to guard in sixte.
Starts to step forward, straightening the sword arm.	Attempts to parry counter-sixte. • This first parry is taken relatively early.
Does a counter-disengagement during the step in response to the early parry.	Does a second faster parry of counter-sixte, lightly meeting the blade. • The parry is correctly formed as the opponent's step is completed. Starts to move the hand forward a little as if to riposte, with the blades still in contact. • The fencers are now at straight arm distance to body.
Pressures the blade lightly toward sixte, opposing.	Disengages with the sword arm still bent, then starts to straighten.
Parries counter-sixte and steps backward. • The fencers are now at lunge distance to body.	Counter-disengages and completes the straightening of the sword arm. Starts to lunge.

Does a second parry of counter-sixte.

Counter-disengages progressively during lunge and lightly hits to chest.
Leaves the point on the chest and waits for Fencer A's signal.

Taps the blade on the quarte side as a signal to recover to guard.

Recovers backward to guard, this time in quarte.

Starts to steps forward straightening the sword arm with a disengagement.
Threatens the opponent's open target.

Attempts to parry counter-quarte.
• The first parry is taken relatively early.

Does a counter-disengagement during the step in response to the early parry.

Does a second faster parry of counter-quarte, lightly meeting the blade.
•The parry is correctly formed as the opponent's step is completed.
Starts to move the hand forward a little as if to riposte, with the blades still in contact.
• The fencers are now at straight arm distance to body.

Pressures the blade lightly toward quarte, opposing.

Disengages with the sword arm still bent, then starts to straighten.

Parries counter-quarte and steps backward.
• The fencers are now at lunge distance to body

Counter-disengages and completes the straightening of the sword arm.
Starts to lunge.

Does a second parry of counter-quarte.

Counter-disengages progressively during lunge and lightly hits to chest.

The left-handed/right-handed combination version reads as follows. Fencer B starts covered

Fencer A	Fencer B
In sixte. Pressures the blade lightly toward quarte.	In sixte. Disengages and starts to lunge.
Parries counter-quarte.	Does a counter-disengagement progressively during lunge and lightly hits to chest. Leaves the point on the chest and waits for Fencer A's signal.
Taps the blade on the sixte side as a signal to recover to guard.	Recovers backward to guard in sixte.
Starts to step forward, straightening the sword arm.	Attempts to parry counter-sixte. • This first parry is taken relatively early.
Does a counter-disengagement during the step in response to the early parry.	Does a second faster parry of counter-sixte, lightly meeting the blade. • The parry is correctly formed as the opponent's step is completed. Starts to move the hand forward a little as if to riposte, with the blades still in contact. • The fencers are now at straight arm distance to body.
Pressures the blade lightly toward quarte, opposing.	Disengages with sword arm still bent, then starts to straighten.
Parries counter-quarte and steps backward. • The fencers are now at lunge distance to body.	Counter-disengages and completes the straightening of the sword arm. Starts to lunge.
Does a second parry of counter-quarte.	Counter-disengages progressively during lunge and lightly hits to chest. • Leaves the point on the chest and waits for Fencer A's signal.

Taps the blade on the sixte side as a signal to recover to guard.

Recovers backward to guard, this time in quarte.

Starts to steps forward, straightening the sword arm with a disengagement.
Threatens the opponent's open target.

Attempts to parry counter-quarte.
• The first parry is taken relatively early.

Does a counter-disengagement during the step in response to the early parry.

Does a second faster parry of counter-quarte, lightly meeting the blade.
• The parry is correctly formed as the opponent's step is completed.
Starts to move the hand forward a little as if to riposte, with the blades still in contact.
• The fencers are now at straight arm distance to body.

Pressures the blade lightly toward sixte, opposing.

Disengages with the sword arm still bent then starts to straighten.

Parries counter-sixte and steps backward.
• The fencers are now at lunge distance to body

Counter-disengages and completes the straightening of the sword arm.
Starts to lunge.

Does a second parry of counter-sixte.

Counter-disengages progressively during lunge and lightly hits to chest.

Counter-Ripostes

Start at lunge distance to body with the blades engaged. A counter-riposte training/coaching routine is also included in Chapter 3.

A direct counter-riposte:

Fencer A	**Fencer B**
1 In sixte. Pressures the blade lightly toward sixte.	In sixte. Steps forward and straightens the sword arm with a disengagement. The point is just short of the target. • The fencers are now at straight arm distance to body.
Lightly touches the blade in quarte and ripostes to chest.	Parries quarte and counter-riposte to chest.

(Left-handed/right-handed combination: the opponent's blade is on Fencer B's outside. Fencer B is covered. Fencer A pressures the blade lightly toward quarte, then lightly touches the blade in sixte and ripostes to chest.)

An indirect counter-riposte:

2 In sixte. Pressures the blade lightly toward sixte.	In sixte. Steps forward and straightens the sword arm with a disengagement: as before. • The fencers are now at straight arm distance to body.
Parries in quarte and ripostes as before.	Parries quarte. Starts to move the hand forward a little as if to counter-riposte, with the blades still in contact.
Pressures the blade lightly toward quarte, opposing.	Disengages with the sword arm still bent, then starts to straighten.
Steps backward. • The fencers are now at lunge distance to body.	Completes the straightening of the sword arm and lunges with hit to chest.

For an alternative ending, Fencer B can rotate and lower the hand a little into pronation, rather than disengage, and finish with a hit to the low line.

Left-handed/right-handed combination: the opponent's blade is on

Fencer B's outside. Fencer B is covered. Fencer A pressures the blade lightly toward quarte, parries sixte and ripostes as before, then pressures the blade lightly toward sixte, opposing.)

Next, start at lunge distance to body with absence of blade.

A compound counter-riposte:

3 In sixte.
Gives agreed signal for the training sequence to begin.

Parries counter-sixte and pauses briefly.
• The circular action of the point should be as small as possible.
• Fencer A is looking for an open or opening line.

Riposts with lunge to the low line.

Attempts to take the blade on either side as the counter-riposte develops.
Recovers to guard in either sixte or quarte.
• The fencers are now at lunge distance to body.

In octave
Does straight thrust from absence of blade to the high line.

Recovers backward to sixte.
• The fencers are now at lunge distance to body.

Parries octave and starts to counter-riposte with a feint to chest.

Deceives the blade and lunges with the hit to chest.

An angulated counter-riposte:

4 In sixte.
Gives agreed signal for the training sequence to begin.

Parries quarte.

In octave
Does straight thrust from absence of blade to the high line.

Quickly recovers backward to guard, anticipating the riposte, steps backward a little.
The distance between the two

	fencers is now a little further than lunge distance to body.
Ripostes with flèche, carefully running past the opponent without contact.	Parries counter-sixte, holds on to the blade and does an angulated riposte to upper back as the opponent runs past.

(Left-handed/right-handed combination: parries counter-quarte, holds on to the blade and does an angulated riposte to body as the opponent runs past on the outside of the defender's sword arm.)

Following is a training exercise at lunge distance to body starting with absence of blade:

Fencer A	**Fencer B**
1 In octave. Does straight thrust from absence of blade to the high line.	In sixte. Parries quarte.
Pressures the blade lightly toward quarte and recovers backward to guard in quarte.	Disengages and ripostes with lunge to chest, riposting into the opening line.
Parries sixte and begins to move the hand forward a little as if riposting into the high line, still holding on to the blade.	Recovers to guard in sixte.
Lunges into the low line, riposting into the open line.	Parries octave.
Pressures the blade lightly toward octave and recovers backward to guard in octave.	Lifts the point and lunges into the high line, riposting into the open line.
Parries sixte and begins to move the hand forward a little as if to riposte, still holding on to the blade.	Recovers to guard in quarte.
Lunges into the high line,	Parries counter-quarte.

riposting into the opening line.

Pressures the blade lightly toward quarte, staying on the lunge. • Fencer A's target is now at straight arm distance to body.	Disengages with the sword arm still bent, then straightens arm with hit to chest, riposting into the opening line.

(Left-handed/right-handed combination: Fencer A first pressures the blade lightly toward sixte and recovers backward to guard in sixte. Then parries quarte and begins to move the hand forward a little as if riposting into the high line, still holding on to the blade. Later, pressures the blade lightly toward septime and recovers backward to guard in septime. Then parries quarte and begins to move the hand forward a little as if to riposte, still holding on to the blade. Later, pressures the blade lightly toward sixte, staying on the lunge.)

A pronated parry can be introduced into a sequence.
Start at lunge distance to body with absence of blade.

Fencer A	**Fencer B**
1 In sixte. Gives agreed signal for the training sequence to begin.	In octave. Does straight thrust from absence of blade.
Parries quarte and ripostes to chest.	Parries quarte on the lunge and counter-ripostes to chest. • Keep the point low, pointing to the chest. • Imagine that you are parrying with your elbow.

Next we can introduce a little mobility.

2 In sixte. Gives agreed signal for the training sequence to begin.	In octave. Does straight thrust from absence of blade.
Parries quarte and starts to riposte.	Recovers backward to guard in sixte. • The fencers are now at lunge distance to body.

Ripostes with lunge to chest.
- The fencers are now at straight arm distance to body.

Parries quarte and counter-riposte to chest.
- Do not attempt to parry and counter-riposte until you have fully recovered to guard.
- Try not to lean forward or backward, after the recovery.

Now try a new development.

3   In sixte.
Gives agreed signal for the training sequence to begin.

In octave.
Does straight thrust from absence of blade.

Parries quarte.

Recovers to guard in sixte.
- The fencers are now at lunge distance to body

Steps in to close quarters, trying to angulate around the antici-pated parry of quarte.
- The fencers are now at straight arm distance to body.

Parries a high prime and care-fully places the counter-riposte on the target by lifting point.

(Left-handed/right-handed combination: Fencer B parries counter-sixte instead of quarte for 1. and 2. For 3., Fencer A might wish to parry quarte, then step in at close quarters, trying to angulate around Fencer B's guard in sixte. Fencer B can parry tierce then counter-riposte.)

For the next session start at lunge distance to body with absence of blade.

Fencer A

Fencer B

1   In sixte.
Gives agreed signal for the training sequence to begin.

In octave.
Does straight thrust from absence of blade

Parries counter-sixte and starts to riposte.

Recovers to guard in sixte.
- The fencers are now at lunge distance to body.

Ripostes with lunge to the low line, pronating the hand.

Parries octave and counter-ripostes to chest.

2 In sixte.
Gives agreed signal for the training sequence to begin.

Parries counter-sixte and starts to riposte.

Steps in to close quarters, trying to angulate around the antici-pated parry of octave.
• The fencers are now at straight arm distance to body.

In octave.
Does straight thrust from absence of blade

Recovers to guard in sixte.
• The fencers are now at lunge distance to body

Parries seconde and places the counter-riposte by angulating and holding on to the blade. Rotates the hand into prona-tion, while opposing the oppo-nent's blade at the same time.

3 In sixte.
Gives agreed signal for the training sequence to begin.

Parries counter-sixte and starts to riposte.

Lunges to top shoulder with the riposte.

In octave.
Does straight thrust from absence of blade.

Recovers to guard in sixte, but with top of the shoulder a little exposed.
• The fencers are now at lunge distance to body

Parries tierce and counter-ripostes to flank.
• The parry opposes the oppo-nent's blade.

(Left-handed/right-handed combination: in 1., 2.and 3., parries quarte instead of counter-sixte. Following the parry of tierce the riposte is to chest.)

4 In sixte.
Gives agreed signal for the training sequence to begin.

Parries quarte and starts to riposte.

In octave.
Does straight thrust from absence of blade

Immediately parries quinte, still on the lunge, and does a croisé to flank.
• The hand should be well for-ward in quinte.

(Left-handed/right-handed combination: Fencer A parries counter-sixte instead of quarte. The croisé finishes to chest.)

Compound Attacks

Many compound attacks will be launched from absence of blade. The final line of the attack will depend on the opponent's reaction and the inclinations of the attacker. Although it seems unlikely that a fencer will not respond in some way to a threat of attack, a 'no response' option is helpful in starting a training routine.

Start at lunge distance to body with absence of blade.

Fencer A	**Fencer B**
1 In sixte. Gives agreed signal for the training sequence to begin.	In octave. In own time, lifts the point and starts to lunge slowly to chest.
Does not respond.	Finishes with hit to chest, accelerating into the finish. • The attack at first starts slowly, but gains momentum as the action continues, until it is fastest at the finish.
2 In sixte. Gives agreed signal for the training sequence to begin.	In octave. In own time, lifts the point and starts to lunge slowly to chest with the feint.
Attempts to parry late during the course of the opponent's lunge, either quarte, counter-sixte, or octave.	Evades the blade during the course of the lunge and finishes with a hit to chest. • Try to ensure that the blades do not touch.

Having mastered each of the above, Fencer A can vary the responses, including the 'no response' training option.

A fencer is vulnerable to attack when stepping forward. To get your opponent to advance, try stepping backward. Start at lunge distance to body with the blades engaged.

3 In sixte.	In sixte.

Gives agreed signal for the training sequence to begin.	In own time, steps backward. • The fencers are now at step and lunge distance to body.
When ready, steps forward in response, following. • Fencer A is vulnerable while stepping forward. • The fencers are now at lunge distance to body.	Straightens arm and lunges to chest as Fencer A completes the step.
Attempts to parry during the course of the opponent's lunge, either quarte, counter-sixte, or octave.	Evades the blade during the course of the lunge and finishes with a hit to chest. • In a real situation this would be used as a surprise attack, employed only occasionally.

(Left-handed/right-handed combination: the opponent's blade is on Fencer B's outside. Fencer B is covered.)

Next, repeat the previous exercise but introduce a cutover instead of the disengagement, or revert to low line following the evasion of the blade. Evading the blade is sometimes called a 'trompement' – a deception of the opponent's attempt to parry.

The next compound attack is a double cutover. Done properly, it should flow forward continuously with no break in the timing. Start at lunge distance to body with the blades engaged.

Fencer A	**Fencer B**
In sixte. Pressures the blade lightly toward sixte.	In sixte. Steps forward and straightens the sword arm with a cutover. • Be careful not to draw the arm back and invite a stop-hit. • Move the hand before the foot.
Steps backward immediately to avoid being hit. • The fencers are once again at lunge distance to body.	Starts to lunge.

Parries quarte early.	Does a second cutover during the course of the lunge and hits to chest.
	• The cutover should just clear the opponent's point.
	• Be careful not to draw the hand back and break the timing.
	• Try not to drop the hand as the hit might land flat, without the character of penetration.

(Left-handed/right-handed combination: the opponent's blade is on Fencer B's outside. Fencer B is covered. Fencer A pressures the blade lightly toward quarte and parries sixte early.)

Another way to put pressure on an opponent is to take the blade and close distance. This has the effect of positioning the attacker's point dangerously close to the defender's target, which often gets a reaction. We will start with a basic training routine and slowly develop an effective compound attack. Fencer A begins by not responding, which is done for training purposes only. Usually a fencer would respond to an impending threat.

Start at lunge distance to body with the blades engaged.

Fencer A	**Fencer B**
1 In sixte.	In sixte.
Gives agreed signal for the training sequence to begin.	In own time, takes a small step forward and pressures on the sixte side of blade.
	• This has the effect of exposing the opponent's target.
	• The step is small and exploratory.
	• The hand action is small and sharp and applied with the landing of the rear foot.
	• The fencers are now at straight arm distance to body.
Does not respond to impending threat.	Straightens arm and finishes with hit to chest, only

lightly bending the blade.
- Make any necessary adjustment to the distance when training to ensure that the fencers do not get too close.

2   In sixte.
Gives agreed signal for the training sequence to begin.

In sixte.
In own time, takes a small step forward and pressures on the sixte side of blade.
- The fencers are now at straight arm distance to body.

Steps backward, returning the pressure.
- The fencers are now at lunge distance to body.

Disengages neatly and lunges with hit to chest.

3   In sixte.
Gives agreed signal for the training sequence to begin.

In sixte.
In own time, takes a small step forward and pressures on the sixte side of blade.
- The fencers are now at straight arm distance to body.

Steps backward, returning the pressure.
- The fencers are now at lunge distance to body.
- The timing and speed of the return pressure can be varied, requiring Fencer B to respond accordingly.

Disengages neatly and starts to lunge with feint to chest.

Parries quarte.
- Fencer A gets caught up in a lateral, side-to-side response.

Disengages progressively during the course of the lunge and hits to chest.

(Left-handed/right-handed combination: the opponent's blade is on Fencer B's outside. Fencer B is covered. Fencer A's target is exposed at the outset, but is further exposed by the pressure on the inside of the blade. After Fencer A's return of pressure the parry is sixte.)

A fencer who holds the blade (upwards) in sixte can be vulnerable to beat attacks. Some prefer to keep the blade horizontal while fencing, with the point often next to the opponent's guard. It is harder to do a beat attack on this kind of blade presentation. A nice low–high compound attack can be launched from this position with minimal movements around the defender's guard.

Start with Fencer B's point adjacent to the opponent's guard in the five o'clock position.

Fencer A	**Fencer B**
1 In sixte. Gives agreed signal for the training sequence to begin.	In sixte, but holding blade parallel to the floor, places the point in the five o'clock position next to the guard.
Slowly does a parry of octave, as small an action as possible.	Practises rotating the point around the guard without touching, as small an action as possible.
2 In sixte. Gives agreed signal for the training sequence to begin.	In sixte, but holding blade parallel to the floor, places the point in the five o'clock position next to the guard, then starts to lunge.
Quickly parries octave.	Disengages during lunge and hits to chest. • Be careful to adjust your distance so that the attacker's blade just bends.

Once a fencer is attuned to a particular action they will tend to anticipate.

3 In sixte. Gives agreed signal for the training sequence to begin.	Starts in sixte, but suddenly places point in the five o'clock position next to the guard.
Parries octave, anticipating.	Disengages during lunge and lunges with hit to chest, just bending the blade.

(Left-handed/right-handed combination: places point in the seven o'clock position next to the guard.)

The same exercise can be performed by Fencer A attempting to gather the blade from below the guard with counter-sixte. Start as before by practising as small an action as possible. Lastly, both parries can be applied randomly and their timing, fast or slow, early or late, can be varied.

Now with blades engaged at lunge distance to body we can try the classic 'swallow tail' one–two. The 'swallow tail' describes the shape that the hand and blade make during this action. Start with a nice accurate disengagement.

Fencer A	**Fencer B**
1 In sixte. Pressures the blade lightly toward sixte.	In sixte. Disengages and straightens the sword arm. • The fencers are still at lunge distance to body.

(Left-handed/right-handed combination: the opponent's blade is on Fencer B's outside. Fencer B is covered. Fencer A pressures the blade lightly toward quarte.)

A simple attack from this position can be parried with a short quarte parry, or perhaps a small circular motion of counter-sixte. Next, Fencer B angulates the attack. This is done intentionally to draw the parry further out.

2 In sixte. Pressures the blade lightly toward sixte.	In sixte. Disengages and straightens the sword arm and moves the hand across about 150mm towards the opponent's quarte side.

(Left-handed/right-handed combination: the opponent's blade is on Fencer B's outside. Fencer B is covered. Fencer A pressures the blade lightly toward quarte.)

An angulated attack from this side is not easily stopped with a neat counter-sixte, which will not gather the blade, and the opponent's reaction to quarte is likely to be exaggerated because of the element of surprise.

3 In sixte.	In sixte.

Pressures the blade lightly toward sixte.	Disengages and straightens the sword arm and moves the hand out as before, starts to lunge and brings the point back in at the same time, completing the angulated feint.
Parries quarte, wide.	Disengages during the course of the lunge, angles hand in the opposite direction and hits to chest.
	• Having exaggerated the parry of quarte, a successive parry to sixte, particularly against an angulated finish, is extremely difficult.

(Left-handed/right-handed combination: the opponent's blade is on Fencer B's outside. Fencer B is covered. Fencer A pressures the blade lightly toward quarte, then parries sixte.)

The two angulated positions of the blade make the distinctive 'swallow tail' shape. It is hard to do successive parries to this.

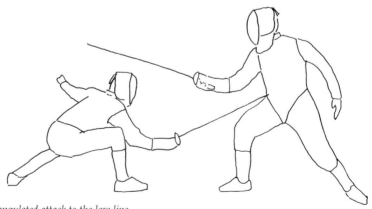

An angulated attack to the low line.

Successive Parries and Ripostes

With successive parries, the first parry is taken early in order to initiate the attacker's change in line. The second parry should be in defence of the final action into a known line. The initial parry need not be fully formed.

This, combined with taking it early, leaves time for the second parry to be correctly formed.

Start on guard with the blades crossed at lunge distance to body. Begin with a circular parry and riposte.

Fencer A	Fencer B
1 In sixte. Disengages and lunges to chest.	In sixte. Parries counter-sixte and ripostes to chest. • Try to keep the parry as small as possible.
2 In sixte. Disengages and lunges to chest.	In sixte. Starts to parry counter-sixte early.
Counter-disengages progressively during the course of the lunge.	Parries quarte and ripostes to chest.

(Left-handed/right-handed combination: in 1. and 2., the opponent's blade is on Fencer B's outside. Fencer B is covered.)

3 In octave. Does straight thrust from absence of blade to high line.	In sixte. Starts to parry counter-sixte early.
Counter-disengages progressively during the course of the lunge.	Parries quarte.
Ducks down on the lunge to make it harder to hit on the chest.	Ripostes lightly to the back.
4 In octave. Does straight thrust from absence of blade to high line.	In sixte. Starts to parry counter-sixte early.
Counter-disengages progressively during the course of the lunge.	Parries octave with a sudden change of direction, lifts the point and ripostes with opposition, the hit landing in the high line.

(Left-handed/right-handed combination: Fencer B's riposte with opposition might be made with angulation to the back.)

The next development is as follows:

5   In octave.
Does straight thrust from
absence of blade to high line.

In sixte.
Starts to parry counter-sixte
early.

Counter-disengages progressively during the course of the
lunge.

Parries octave.

Attempts to recover to guard in
sixte.
• The fencers are once again
  approaching lunge distance to
  body.

Steps in with the riposte, closing the distance.

Parries quarte.
• The fencers are now
  approaching straight arm distance to body.

Ripostes with angulation
around the parry of quarte,
lightly bending the blade.

(Left-handed/right-handed combination: Fencer A attempts to recover to guard in sixte and holds this position. Fencer B ripostes with angulation around sixte, lightly bending the blade.)

The use of a pronated parry can increase the effectiveness of the angulated riposte.

6   In octave.
Does straight thrust from
absence of blade to high line.

In sixte.
Starts to parry counter-sixte
early.

Counter-disengages progressively during the course of the
lunge.

Parries seconde, with a sharp
turn of the wrist.

Attempts to recover to guard in
sixte.
• The fencers are once again
  approaching lunge distance to
  body.

Steps in with the riposte, closing the distance.
• Keep the hand in pronation.

Parries quarte.	Ripostes with increased angulation around the parry of quarte, lightly bending the blade.
• The fencers are now approaching straight arm distance to body.	

(Left-handed/right-handed combination: Fencer A attempts to recover to guard in sixte and holds this position. Fencer B ripostes with angulation around sixte, lightly bending the blade.)

Another development is as follows:

1	In octave. Does straight thrust from absence of blade to high line.	In sixte. Parries quarte and ripostes to chest.

Next, Fencer A will deceive the parry.

2	In octave. Does straight thrust from absence of blade to high line.	In sixte. Starts to parry quarte early.
	Disengages progressively during the course of the lunge. • Be careful not to let the blades touch.	Parries sixte and ripostes to chest.
3	In octave. Does straight thrust from absence of blade to high line.	In sixte. Starts to parry quarte early.
	Disengages progressively during the course of the lunge.	Times thrust through sixte in a single decisive action.

Preparations (Including Attacks au Fer)

Attacks au fer are preparations involving attacks on the blade. These have been listed in the preceding chapter. The double blade preparation which follows starts at lunge distance to body with the blades engaged.

Fencer A	**Fencer B**
1 In sixte.	In sixte.

Does either a long or short pressure on the outside of the opponent's blade.	Returns the pressure like for like, returning to the original position. • Respond with exactly the long or short pressure that Fencer A has used.

(Left-handed/right-handed combination: the opponent's blade is on Fencer B's outside. Fencer B is covered.)

2 In octave.
Does straight thrust from absence of blade to high line.

In sixte.
Parries counter-sixte.

Recovers backward to guard in sixte.
• The fencers are now at lunge distance to body.

Ripostes with coulé to chest, raising the hand suddenly at the last moment, Fencer B's forte opposing Fencer A's foible.

(Left-handed/right-handed combination: Fencer B will parry quarte.)

Next, practise lunge distance to body with the blades engaged.

3 In sixte.
Attempts to take the blade on the outside.

In sixte.
Deceives the blade and engages it in quarte.
• Fencer A's target is now exposed.

As the blade is engaged, applies a return pressure.
• This is a natural reaction to cover the exposed target.
• The fencers are still at lunge distance to body.

As the pressure is applied, disengages and lunges with hit to chest.

(Left-handed/right-handed combination: the opponent's blade is on Fencer B's outside. Fencer B is covered. Fencer A attempts to take the blade on the inside. Fencer B deceives the blade and engages in sixte.)

The following is a double preparation:

4 In sixte.

In octave.

Gives agreed signal for the training sequence to begin.	In own time, takes a small step forward and gathers the blade, engaging it in octave. • Great care must be taken when taking this small step forward as the opponent might attempt to deceive the blade and take the initiative. • A small step allows a little time in which to get in a quick parry if this happens.
Steps backward, releasing the blade from engagement. • The fencers are once again at lunge distance to body.	Steps forward and engages the blade in sixte. • Fencer B is putting on the pressure. • The second preparation can be taken a little faster.
Steps backward and applies a pressure, reacting. • The fencers are once again at lunge distance to body.	Disengages and lunges with hit to chest.

(Left-handed/right-handed combination: the opponent's blade is on Fencer B's outside. Fencer B is covered.)

The next exercise is a double preparation with a compound finish, starting at lunge distance to body.

5	In sixte. Gives agreed signal for the training sequence to begin.	In octave. In own time, takes a small step forward and gathers the blade, engaging it in octave.
	Steps backward, releasing the blade from engagement. • The fencers are once again at lunge distance to body.	Steps forward and engages the blade in sixte.
	Steps backward and applies a pressure, reacting. • The fencers are once again at lunge distance to body.	Disengages and starts to lunge.

Parries quarte.	Disengages during the course of the lunge hits to chest.

(Left-handed/right-handed combination: the opponent's blade is on Fencer B's outside. Fencer B is covered. Fencer A parries sixte at the finish.)

The next starts at lunge distance to body with the blades engaged.

6	In sixte. Gives agreed signal for the training sequence to begin.	In sixte. In own time, takes a small step forward, engaging the blade sharply in tierce. • The wrist turns from supination to pronation.
	Steps backward and applies a pressure, reacting. • The fencers are once again at lunge distance to body.	Disengages and lunges with hit to chest.

(Left-handed/right-handed combination: the opponent's blade is on Fencer B's outside. Fencer B is covered. Fencer B might wish to consider finishing with a hit to flank.)

7	In sixte. Gives agreed signal for the training sequence to begin.	In sixte. In own time, steps forward, engaging the blade sharply in tierce.
	As the opponent engages, suddenly disengages. • Fencer B is courting danger.	Parries quinte. • Keep the hand well forward in quinte. • Fencer B's step has to be sufficiently short to allow time for the parry to be formed.
	Steps backward, retreating. • The fencers are once again at lunge distance to body.	Lunges with hit to flank with opposition.

(Left-handed/right-handed combination: the opponent's blade is on Fencer B's outside. Fencer B is covered. Fencer B finishes with hit to chest with opposition.)

8 In sixte. Gives agreed signal for the training sequence to begin.	In octave. Steps forward and begins to engage the blade in sixte.
Steps backward. • The fencers are once again at lunge distance to body.	Changes the engagement to quarte, lunges down the blade with opposition and hits to chest.

Now try some beats at lunge distance to body. The fencers start from absence of blade. Practise this hand action.

Fencer A	**Fencer B**
1 In sixte. Gives agreed signal for the training sequence to begin.	In octave. Slowly lifts the point to directly below guard without touching, then suddenly snaps the hand clockwise or counter-clockwise to perform beat in centre of blade. • The beat is applied by using the fingers.

Next, add in a lunge:

2 In sixte. Gives agreed signal for the training sequence to begin.	In octave. Slowly lifts the point as before, then suddenly snaps the hand with a beat and lunges with hit to chest.
3 In sixte. Gives agreed signal for the training sequence to begin.	In octave. Slowly lifts the point as before, then suddenly snaps the hand with a beat and starts to lunge.
Parries quarte or sixte.	Disengages during the course of the lunge and hits to chest.

Next, a beat attack used tactically.

Fencer A	**Fencer B**
1 In octave.	In sixte.

Does straight thrust from absence of blade.	Steps backward to avoid being hit.
Recovers backward to guard but leaves the arm straight.	Steps forward and attempts to take the blade either side. • The fencers are once again at lunge distance to body.
Does a dérobement to evade the blade. • It is important that the blades do not touch. • Fencer A is awarded the hit.	Lunges and lightly hits to chest.

Fencer B has just lost. Now the tables will be turned. A beat attack can be very effective in the middle of a fencing sequence. If the beat is executed correctly, then Fencer A should not be able to do a second dérobement. Fencer B's first attempt to take the blade should be slow. By contrast, the beat should be a sudden surprise action.

2	In octave. Does straight thrust from absence of blade.	In sixte. Steps backward to avoid being hit.
	Recovers backward to guard, but leaves the arm straight.	Steps forward, slowly attempts to take the blade either side. • This time, Fencer B anticipates the dérobement. • The fencers are once again at lunge distance to body.
	Does a dérobement.	Beats the blade and lunges with point to chest. • Fencer B is awarded the hit.

The fencers start from absence of blade at lunge distance to body.

Fencer A	**Fencer B**
1 In sixte. Gives agreed signal for the training sequence to begin.	In octave. Slowly lifts the point and starts to straighten the sword arm as if launching an attack, then suddenly pulls the hand back to sixte.

Straightens the sword arm, reacting to the sudden withdrawal of the hand. • The fencers are still at lunge distance to body. • Fencer A is attempting to gain priority.	Beats the blade and lunges with point to chest.

2	In sixte. Gives agreed signal for the training sequence to begin.	In octave. Slowly lifts the point and starts to straighten the sword arm as if launching an attack, then suddenly pulls hand back to sixte.

Straightens the sword arm, reacting to the sudden withdrawal of the hand. • The fencers are still at lunge distance to body.	Beats the blade on the quarte side and starts to lunge.

Parries quarte, reacting to the beat.	Disengages during the course of the lunge and hits to chest.

Attacks on the Preparation

Start at step and lunge distance to body.

Fencer A	**Fencer B**

1	In sixte. Steps forward. • The fencers are now at lunge distance to body.	In sixte. Lunges with point to chest into the opponent's preparation.

Now at lunge distance to body with the blades engaged.

2	In sixte. Gives agreed signal for the training sequence to begin.	In sixte. Steps backward. • The fencers are now at step and lunge distance to body.
	• Fencer B is now too far away to hit with a lunge.	Lunges with point to chest into the opponent's preparation.

In own time, Fencer A steps forward in order to close the distance and launch an attack.

Next, start at lunge distance to body with the blades engaged.

3   In sixte.   In sixte.
Changes the engagement from   Counter-disengages and lunges
sixte to quarte.   with hit to chest into the opponent's preparation.

Next time, Fencer A applies second intention and introduces a parry and
riposte.

4   In sixte.   In sixte.
Changes the engagement from   Counter-disengages and
sixte to quarte.   attempts to lunge to chest into
the opponent's preparation.

Parries and ripostes.
• Select your own parry.

The way is now clear for Fencer B to launch a compound attack on the
opponent's preparation.

5   In sixte.   In sixte.
Changes the engagement from   Counter-disengages and
sixte to quarte.   attempts to lunge to chest into
the opponent's preparation.

Attempts to do a simple parry.   Disengages during the course
of the lunge and hits to chest.

(Left-handed/right-handed combination: with 2., 3., 4. and 5., the opponent's blade is on Fencer B's outside. Fencer B is covered. Fencer A rotates
under the blade trying to adopt a covered position in sixte.)

Next, at lunge distance to body:

6   In octave.   In sixte.
Lifts the point and beats the   Immediately returns the beat
blade crisply in the centre of the   and lunges with a hit to chest.
blade.   • Keep the beats as neat as possible.

- Ensure that the arm is straight before the lunge is made.
- Hand moves before the foot.

Now from a little further apart:

7   In sixte.
    Does a balestra.
    - Adjust your distance a little until the fencers are at lunge distance to body after Fencer A's balestra.

In sixte.
Does a beat attack and lunges with hit to chest.

At lunge distance to body:

8   In octave.
    Gives agreed signal for the training sequence to begin.

    Takes large step forward and attempts to take the blade.

In sixte.
Straightens arm.

Does a dérobement with hit to chest.
- The fencers end up at straight arm distance to body.
- The blade should only lightly bend.
- Adjust the distance if required.

Prise de Fer Actions

Prise de fer actions can be done offensively or defensively.
    Start at lunge distance to body.

Fencer A

Fencer B

1   In octave.
    Does a straight thrust from absence of blade to the high line and stays on the lunge.

In sixte.
Parries quarte and ripostes with croisé to flank.

2   In octave.
    Does beat attack from absence of blade to the high line.

In sixte.
Parries quarte, ripostes with croisé.

(Left-handed/right-handed combination: for 1. and 2., Fencer B ripostes with croisé to chest.)

Now do a bind. Start at lunge distance to body with absence of blade.

Fencer A	**Fencer B**
1 In sixte. Straightens the sword arm.	In octave. Takes the blade in quarte, then moves the hand diagonally to octave (forte to foible) and finishes by lunging with opposition into the high line. • Do the bind in one smooth, continuous action

(Left-handed/right-handed combination: try finishing to the flank.)

Next, Fencer A offers either a straight arm, to which the offensive response is a bind, or lunges with a simple attack, to which the defensive response is a croisé.

A molinello has been included in this section as it is primarily based on a prime-tierce bind. It can be a prise de fer, but has other versatile applications which will be explained. It is made in one movement and reaches the target via a circular route. At sabre, it is a circular cut at head or chest, passing through the prime position. This action can be used at foil and sabre, but not épée, where the vulnerability of the extended target can lead to problems. Interestingly, it can be performed with or without contact with the opponent's blade. Used as a parry, is a very good response to angulated attacks.

The hand starts in a prime-like position. This is a little lower than the high (foil) prime parry discussed earlier. The hand is level with the blade of the extended arm. The cutover type action which follows is carried through by a rotating hand and wrist action. The blade does a complete circular rotation and the arm ends up straight, with the point moving forward toward the target. The trick here is to take the hand back a little during the rotation to land with the point. This can be used as a prise de fer (taking the blade), a beat, a simple or compound attack and as a riposte. A cutover riposte like this is sometimes called a flying riposte, a term which also applies to cutover ripostes from low-line parries.

Start at step and lunge distance to body.

Fencer A	**Fencer B**
1 In sixte. Straightens the sword arm.	In sixte. Steps forward and lightly engages the blade through prime. • The fencers are now at lunge distance to body. Does a cutover attack and lunges with the point to chest.
2 In sixte. Straightens the sword arm.	In sixte. Steps forward and beats the blade through prime. • The fencers are now at lunge distance to body. Does a cutover attack and lunges with the point to chest.
3 In sixte. Gives agreed signal for the training sequence to begin.	In sixte. Steps forward, rotating the hand through prime. • The fencers are now at lunge distance to body. Does a cutover attack and lunges with the point to chest. • This time there is no blade contact.
4 In sixte. Gives agreed signal for the training sequence to begin. Steps back a little to just outside lunge distance. • This is between lunge distance and step and lunge distance to body.	In sixte. Steps forward and starts to rotate the hand through prime. • The fencers are now at lunge distance to body. • Fencer B cannot reach the opponent with a lunge, but can with a flèche. Flèches with the point to chest. • Be careful to run past your opponent without making physical contact.

At lunge distance to body we can try a flying riposte.

Fencer A	Fencer B
1 In octave. Does straight thrust from absence of blade.	In sixte. Parries prime with guard only a little above the foible of the attacking blade, then starts to riposte with the flying cutover.
Recovers backward to sixte. • The fencers are once again at lunge distance to body.	Finishes the flying cutover and straightens arm, then lunges with the point to chest. • This action must be smooth and continuous.
2 In octave. Does straight thrust from absence of blade.	In sixte. Parries prime with guard only a little above the foible of the attacking blade, then starts to riposte with the flying cutover feint to chest. • Make the feint as realistic as possible.
Recovers backward to sixte. • The fencers are once again at lunge distance to body. Parries a high quarte, anticipating.	Finishes the flying cutover and lunges with the point to flank. • This is a compound riposte.

(Left-handed/right-handed combination: Fencer B finishes in the low line.)

Ceding and Opposition Parries

Ceding parries are primarily quarte and prime, plus sixte with a left-handed/right-handed combination. Start at lunge distance to body.

Fencer A	Fencer B
1 In sixte. Gives agreed signal for the training sequence to begin.	In octave. Does a straight thrust from absence of blade to the high line.

	Stays on the lunge.
Parries counter-sixte and extends the sword arm immediately. • This is an envelopment.	Cedes to prime still on the lunge and ripostes directly to chest.

2	In sixte. Gives agreed signal for the training sequence to begin.	In octave. Steps forward and straightens the sword arm. • The fencers are now at straight arm distance to body.
	Envelopes through counter-sixte.	Cedes to prime and ripostes to chest. • This is an action of second intention.

A typical left-handed/right-handed combination follows:

1	In sixte. Gives agreed signal for the training sequence to begin.	In octave. Steps forward and straightens the sword arm. • The fencers are now at straight arm distance to body.
	Envelopes through counter-sixte.	Cedes by rotating hand to sixte and ripostes to chest.

Opposition parries, like all parries, oppose forte to foible:

Fencer A	**Fencer B**
1 In sixte. Gives agreed signal for the training sequence to begin.	In octave. Does a straight thrust from absence of blade to the high line. Stays on the lunge.
Envelopes through counter-sixte.	Opposes to sixte still on the lunge and ripostes to chest.
2 In sixte. Gives agreed signal for the	In octave. Steps forward and straightens

training sequence to begin.	the sword arm. • The fencers are now at straight arm distance to body.
Envelopes through counter-sixte.	Opposes to sixte and ripostes to chest. • This is an action of second intention.

(Left-handed/right-handed combination: Fencer B opposes to quarte.)

Use of the Line

This is largely about the use of the dérobement, where the defender has arm extended with the point aimed directly at the upper portion of the valid target. The attacker attempts to take the blade and the defender deceives it.

Start at lunge distance to body.

Fencer A	**Fencer B**
1 In octave. Gives agreed signal for the training sequence to begin.	In sixte. Straightens the sword arm, pointing directly to the upper valid target area.
Attempts to take the blade.	Does a small dérobement. • It is important that the blades do not touch.
After failure to take the blade, lunges and hits lightly on the target.	Fencer B's point lands on target. • Fencer B is awarded the hit.

Next, start with blades engaged:

2 In sixte. Gives agreed signal for the training sequence to begin.	In sixte. Disengages and does a short lunge, not touching target. • This is an exploratory attack; Fencer A is looking for some kind of a reaction.

Fencer A wishes to take a late parry, so does not respond.	Recovers to guard with the arm straight and pointing directly to the upper valid target area.
Attempts to take the blade.	Does a small dérobement.
After failure to take the blade, lunges and hits lightly on the target.	Fencer B's point lands on target. • Fencer B is awarded the hit.

The next example requires Fencer B to vary the response following observation of the opponent's blade action. Start at lunge distance to body.

3	In octave. Gives agreed signal for the training sequence to begin.	In sixte. Straightens the sword arm, pointing directly to the upper valid target area.
	Attempts to take the blade either on the sixte side, quarte side, on top, or underneath the blade. • This can be done in any order; start slowly, then later vary the speed.	Does a small dérobement, in response to each particular blade action.
	Lunges and hits lightly on the target.	Fencer B's point lands on target. • Fencer B is awarded the hit.

The line can be used as second intention. Start at lunge distance to body.

4	In octave. Gives agreed signal for the training sequence to begin.	In sixte. Straightens the sword arm, pointing directly to the upper valid target area.
	Does a beat attack on the blade and lunges.	Parries and ripostes. • The parry and riposte can also be done tactically, after a

successful dérobement, when the opponent launches a beat attack to recover the initiative.
- The use of the parry and riposte is second intention.

Following is another response to the beat attack:

5 In octave. Gives agreed signal for the training sequence to begin.	In sixte. Straightens the sword arm, pointing directly to the upper valid target area.
Does a beat attack on the quarte side of the blade and lunges.	Rotates the hand through a counter-sixte action with a slight bend in the arm, finishing with the arm completely straight. • This has the effect of blocking out Fencer A's attack, and is called a time thrust.

Imagine a situation where Fencer A has retreated to nearly the end of the piste. To go off the end of the piste will mean losing a hit. The pressure is on to regain ground and Fencer B continues to edge forward. Start at lunge distance to body.

Fencer A	**Fencer B**
In octave. Gives agreed signal for the training sequence to begin.	In sixte. Steps forward and straightens the sword arm.
Steps backward now tenuously close to the end of the piste. • The fencers are at lunge distance to body. Suddenly Fencer A attempts to take the blade with a step forward.	Does a small dérobement and lightly hits with point to chest. • The fencers are at straight arm distance to body.

Fencer A can either take one or two attempts to engage the blade. Fencer B evades the blade once or twice. To evade the blade twice is a compound dérobement.

Counter-Attacks and Responses to Them

Successful counter-offensive actions occur a period of fencing time (the time taken to perform a parry or a step) ahead of the attack. A stop-hit is uncovered (the blade is not met). If the blade is met with opposition, then this is called a time-hit.

Practise the following at straight arm distance to body with a light engagement of the blades.

Fencer A	**Fencer B**
1 In sixte. Withdraws the hand a little. • Fencer B reacts by straightening the sword arm.	In sixte. Straightens the sword arm with a hit to chest, practising a stop-hit.

Then at lunge distance to body:

Fencer A	**Fencer B**
2 In sixte. Steps forward and withdraws the hand. • The fencers are once again at straight arm distance to body.	In sixte. Straightens the sword arm with a stop-hit to chest.

(Left-handed/right-handed combination: for 1. and 2., the opponent's blade is on Fencer B's outside. Fencer B is covered.)

Another choice of hand movement at straight arm distance to body:

Fencer A	**Fencer B**
1 In sixte. Disengages and straightens the sword arm. • In this case, the point is extending toward the opponent's target, so Fencer B responds with a parry, conceding that Fencer A has right of way.	In sixte. Parries and ripostes.

Then at lunge distance to body:

2	In sixte.	In sixte.
	Steps forward, disengages and straightens the sword arm.	Parries and ripostes.
	• The fencers are now at straight arm distance to body.	

(Left-handed/right-handed combination: for 1. and 2., the opponent's blade is on Fencer B's outside. Fencer B is covered.)

Next what happens is Fencer B has to choose the correct response between these two very different hand actions, either responding to the withdrawal of the hand or the straightening of the sword arm with a disengagement.

Another approach is to evade the attack by ducking below the blade, or side-stepping, to avoid the hit landing. Moving the target to avoid an attack is called displacement. When you duck under the blade lift your point a little. If you are too obvious, your opponent may try to hit your back.

Ducking below the blade. A stop-hit known as the 'boar's thrust'.

A flèche attack to the back.

Start at lunge distance to body.

Fencer A	**Fencer B**
1 In octave. Lunges with an attack to the high line.	In sixte. Ducks down below the point and does stop-hit to low line. • Only Fencer B's hit lands.

With the side step, the front foot does not move. The rear foot side steps and the blade angles in toward the opponent's target.

2 In octave. Lunges with an attack to the high line.	In sixte. Does a side step by moving rear foot in direction of sixte and does a stop-hit. • Only Fencer B's hit lands.
3 In octave. Lunges with an attack to the high line.	In sixte. Does a side step by moving rear foot in direction of sixte and does a time-hit, opposing blade through quarte.
4 In octave. Lunges with an attack to the high line.	In sixte. Does a time trust through counter-sixte and hits immediately with point to chest.

(Left-handed/right-handed combination: side-stepping with opposition is likely to be more effective.)

If you can anticipate where the final line is you can even use a time thrust against a one–two attack. Simply parry quarte, early, then time thrust through sixte.

Following are some responses at lunge distance to body, with the blades engaged:

Fencer A	**Fencer B**
In sixte. Gives agreed signal for the training sequence to begin.	In sixte. Starts to step forward with a disengagement, then suddenly withdraws the hand.
Straightens the sword arm immediately, attempting a stop-hit.	Parries quarte and ripostes with a hit to chest.

(Left-handed/right-handed combination: the opponent's blade is on Fencer B's outside. Fencer B is covered. Fencer B straightens the sword arm (without a disengagement), then parries sixte and ripostes with a hit to chest.)

Now some responses to counter-attacks. Start at lunge distance to body with the blades engaged.

	Fencer A	**Fencer B**
1	In sixte. Gives agreed signal for the training sequence to begin.	In sixte. Takes a small step forward and attempts to engage the blade in quarte, with a change of engagement.
	Counter-disengages and straightens the sword arm. • The fencers are now at straight arm distance to body.	Parries sixte, or counter-quarte, and ripostes with hit to chest.

(Left-handed/right-handed combination: the opponent's blade is on Fencer B's outside. Fencer B is covered.)

2   In sixte.
Gives agreed signal for the
training sequence to begin.

In sixte.
Disengages and starts to lunge
with bent arm, inviting a
counter-attack.

Straightens the sword arm,
reacting.

Does beat parry and riposte
during lunge and finishes with
a hit to chest.

(Left-handed/right-handed combination: the opponent's blade is on Fencer B's outside. Fencer B is covered. Fencer B starts to lunge without a disengagement.)

3   In sixte.
Gives agreed signal for the
training sequence to begin.

In sixte.
Starts to cutover slowly, then
suddenly withdraws the hand.

Straightens the sword arm,
reacting.

Does a beat attack and lunges
with a hit to chest.

(Left-handed/right-handed combination: the opponent's blade is on Fencer B's outside. Fencer B is covered.)

Broken Time

Broken time is a form of compound attack that relies on the defender's temporary freezing of reactions. It is used against the defender who parries late, or who parries wildly. When the point is pulled back, it should be held just below the opponent's guard, without touching.

The position is lunge distance to body with the blades engaged. Try these routines progressively.

Fencer A

Fencer B

1   In sixte.
Gives agreed signal for the
training sequence to begin.

In sixte.
Disengages and lunges with a
hit to chest.

Next, introduce a late parry.

2   In sixte.
Gives agreed signal for the
training sequence to begin.

In sixte.
Disengages and lunges with a
hit to chest.

Parries quarte, deliberately late,
and ripostes with hit to chest.

Now we are poised to attempt a broken-time attack.

3	In sixte.	In sixte.
	Gives agreed signal for the training sequence to begin.	Disengages and starts to lunge with a hit to chest.
	Starts to parry quarte, deliberately late.	Pulls back the point, bending the arm on the lunge, placing the point just below the opponent's guard.
		The front foot lands.
		Stays on the lunge.
		• Be careful not to touch the guard.
	Pauses in quarte.	As Fencer A pauses, finishes with a hit to chest.
4	In sixte.	In sixte.
	Gives agreed signal for the training sequence to begin.	Disengages and starts to lunge with a hit to chest.
	Starts to parry quarte, deliberately late.	Pulls back the point, bending the arm on the lunge, placing the point just below the opponent's guard.
		The front foot lands.
		Stays on the lunge.
	Either moves the hand to sixte or stays in quarte.	Finishes with a hit to chest.

Left-handed/right-handed combination: the opponent's blade is on Fencer B's outside. Fencer B is covered. Fencer B straightens the sword arm and lunges with a hit to chest.)

Now practise a choice reaction lesson at lunge distance. Taking the hand back during an attack can evoke different responses and lead to different consequences, so be cautious. Start at lunge distance to body with the blades engaged.

Fencer A	Fencer B
1 In sixte. Gives agreed signal for the training sequence to begin.	In sixte. Steps forward.
Steps backward immediately. • The fencers are once again at lunge distance to body.	Disengages and lunges with a hit to chest. Pulls the hand back, this time with the point raised and the arm bent. The front foot lands. Stays on the lunge.
Does not react.	Finishes with a hit to chest.

Or try the following:

2 In sixte. Gives agreed signal for the training sequence to begin.	In sixte. Steps forward.
Steps backward immediately and attempts to parry quarte. • The fencers are once again at lunge distance to body.	Disengages and lunges with a hit to chest.

(Left-handed/right-handed combination: the opponent's blade is on Fencer B's outside. Fencer B is covered. Fencer B straightens the sword arm and lunges with a hit to chest.)

This time start at step and lunge distance to body. The next variation is only possible due to what has gone before. What follows is a tactical response.

3 In sixte. Gives agreed signal for the training sequence to begin.	In sixte. Steps forward.
Straightens the sword arm. Fencer A anticipates that the opponent will pull the hand back with the point raised and the arm bent. • The fencers are now at lunge distance to body.	Beats down on top of the opponent's blade and lunges with a hit to chest.

Continuity Hitting

This is good for developing a light hand and the ability to remember more than one action. Try each of these moves separately, then apply them sequentially, accuracy being more important than speed. Strive to ensure that you hit gently, always touching exactly the same spot on the target. Look at the part of the target you wish to hit, then apply the point gently.

Start at lunge distance to body with the blades engaged.

Fencer A	**Fencer B**
1 In sixte. Steps forward and straightens the arm with a disengage. • The fencers are now at straight arm distance to body.	In sixte. Parries quarte, holds on to blade momentarily, then ripostes lightly with a hit to chest. Leaves the point on the chest. • Try not to tense the arm.
Taps the centre of the blade lightly and straightens the sword arm.	Parries quarte.
Applies pressure to the blade.	Disengages, lifting the blade to the same height on the other side, with the arm still bent, then lowers the point and hits to chest in exactly the same spot as before. Leaves the point on the chest.
Disengages and taps on the quarte side of the blade and straightens the sword arm.	Parries quarte.
Steps backward, rotating the blade through counter-sixte. • The fencers are now at lunge distance to body.	Steps forward, counter-disengages and hits carefully in the same spot with a straight arm. Leaves the point on the chest. • The fencers are now at straight arm distance to body.
Steps backward and attempts quarte.	Disengages and steps forward with a hit to chest.

• The fencers are now at lunge distance to body.

Leaves the point on the chest.
• The fencers are now at straight arm distance to body.

Steps backward, moving the hand to sixte.
• The fencers are now at lunge distance to body.

Disengages and straightens the sword arm.

Attempts to take the blade in quarte.

Disengages and lunges with point to chest.

(Left-handed/right-handed combination: the opponent's blade is on Fencer B's outside. Fencer B is covered. Try this with Fencer A stepping backward, rotating the blade through counter-quarte, then moving the hand to sixte–quarte–sixte.)

An angulated riposte.

CHAPTER THREE

Coaching Foil

A Few Thoughts

Coaches wishing to train fencers should adopt the teaching position, to avoid the physical effort of holding the on-guard position for extended periods. This is with an erect posture, body inclined a little forward, sword arm well extended, with the other arm bent. This stance is shorter than the on-guard position, the feet comfortably spaced, the front foot following the line of direction, with the rear foot pointing away at about 45 degrees. The knees should be slightly flexed to ensure mobility. Because this stance is more upright than the on-guard position, the hand holding the weapon is held slightly lower, so as to simulate where it would be if the coach were standing on guard. The coach does not lunge, but instead uses foot movements to cover ground.

In every lesson (all weapons) there can be a period of preparation, then technical and tactical application in more accelerated conditions, followed by time to wind down. Offensive and defensive actions may be alternated, progressing from simple to more compound actions. Fencers must learn to co-ordinate their blade and foot actions, responding correctly to various signals or reactions, to build up a range of programmed responses without conscious thought. For this to work, the coach's signals must be consistent, so that the student's response is consistent. In addition, each signal must be sufficiently different, so that the student does not misread the signal and carry out the wrong response. Timing varies in a real fighting situation. To be good, a lesson should mimic reality. In the same vein, by placing the weapon in the opposite hand, the coach is then able to train students in both the left-handed/right-handed combination, as well as the similar-handed situation.

To construct any good individual topic lesson within a set period of time, teach two examples, then join them together as a reaction lesson. A third example can be kept in reserve.

When demonstrating to a class, the coach stands as a fencer with another fencer as assistant. The assistant will first be taught their part in the demonstration. When ready, the coach will then demonstrate the action. It is not necessary to demonstrate every time, particularly if the assistant appears to need a little more practice. A few perfect examples will give a strong visual signal of how it should be done. If demonstrating an attacking action to a class, stop at the end of the lunge and try to look good.

Students will copy what they see. They learn 60 per cent through watching and 30 per cent from listening.

The following training routine might be useful for summer training. No need to lunge much, just concentrate on hitting with the point. Start at lunge distance to body with the blades engaged.

Fencer A	**Fencer B**
1 In sixte. Disengages and steps in at very close quarters with blade extended.	In sixte. Parries quarte and gently places a hit on the chest with arm still bent. Only enough pressure to register a hit.

(Left-handed/right-handed combination: the opponent's blade is on Fencer B's outside. Fencer B is covered.)

2 In sixte. Disengages and steps in at very close quarters with blade extended.	In sixte. Parries quarte.
Raises the hand.	Rotates the hand 90 degrees and places the hit on the flank with arm still bent.

(Left-handed/right-handed combination: the opponent's blade is on Fencer B's outside. Fencer B is covered. Fencer B rotates the hand 90 degrees and places the hit on the chest.)

Alternate hits to flank and chest:

3 In sixte. Disengages and steps in at very close quarters with blade extended.	In sixte. Parries quarte and gently places a hit on the chest with arm still bent.
Immediately goes for the blade.	Disengages around the blade and places the hit on the chest. • Still at close quarters.
4 In sixte. Disengages and steps in at very	In sixte. Parries quarte and gently places

close quarters with blade extended.

a hit on the chest with arm still bent.

Immediately goes for the blade.

Disengages around the blade and places the hit on the chest.
• Still at close quarters.

Steps backward, lightly touching the blade.
• The fencers are once again at lunge distance to body.

Disengages and lunges with a hit to chest.
• The last action can be done with a sudden increase in speed, but ensure that the fencers are sufficiently far apart when the point lands.
• The blade should only lightly bend.

(Left-handed/right-handed combination: in 3. and 4., the opponent's blade is on Fencer B's outside. Fencer B is covered.)

You can try this same exercise at épée. This time, the hits will be to the top of the arm and the top of the leg, instead of to chest and flank.

One of the most frequently used parries at foil is quarte. The routine that follows is for a first counter-riposte (mainly in quarte) and can be adapted to suit any weapon.

Start at lunge distance to body with the blades engaged.

First, practise the parry and riposte.

Fencer A

Fencer B

1   In sixte.
Gives agreed signal for the training sequence to begin.

In sixte.
Lightly pressures the blade by moving the hand a little toward sixte.

Slowly disengages and lunges to chest, attacking into the opening line.

Practises a perfect quarte riposte.
• The hand should only move across sufficient to take the attacker's point away from the target.
• When parrying, ensure that the defender's point does not drift out, as this will increase

the distance to be covered by the riposte.

Continue to train slowly until both the parry and the riposte are perfectly executed. Now at straight arm distance to body, we will try practising a counter-riposte.

2		Starts with a straight sword arm.
	Practises parrying quarte and riposting.	Parries quarte, holding on to the blade momentarily, then counter-ripostes to chest.

(Left-handed/right-handed combination: Fencer A practises parrying sixte and riposting.)

3		Starts with a straight sword arm. in a three-quarters lunge.
	Practises parrying quarte and riposting.	Parries quarte while still on the lunge, then counter-ripostes to chest. • Keep the point in line with the chest during the parry. • This is an action of second intention.

(Left-handed/right-handed combination: Fencer A practises parrying sixte and riposting.)

Now at lunge distance to body with the blades engaged.

4	In sixte. Lightly pressures the blade by moving hand a little toward sixte.	In sixte. Disengages and lunges to chest.
	Parries quarte and ripostes.	Parries quarte and counter-ripostes immediately while still on the lunge. • This is done as a reflex action.

(Left-handed/right-handed combination: the opponent's blade is on Fencer B's outside. Fencer B is covered. Fencer A moves hand a little toward quarte, then parries sixte and ripostes.)

5 In sixte.
Lightly pressures the blade by
moving the hand a little toward
sixte.

In sixte.
Disengages and does three-
quarters lunge.

Parries quarte and ripostes.

Parries quarte and counter-
ripostes on the lunge. This is
done as second intention.

(Left-handed/right-handed combination: the opponent's blade is on
Fencer B's outside. Fencer B is covered. Fencer A moves hand a little
toward quarte, then parries sixte and ripostes.)

Try this as a choice reaction exercise.

6 In sixte.
Lightly pressures the blade by
moving the hand a little toward
sixte.

In sixte.
Disengages and lunges to chest.

Parries quarte and ripostes.

Parries quarte and counter-
ripostes direct on the lunge, or
indirect, disengaging with the
riposte if the opponent
attempts to parry quarte again.

(Left-handed/right-handed combination: the opponent's blade is on
Fencer B's outside. Fencer B is covered. Fencer A moves hand a little
toward quarte, then parries sixte and ripostes. Occasionally attempts to
parry sixte again.)

7 In sixte.
Lightly pressures the blade by
moving the hand a little toward
sixte.

In sixte.
Disengages and steps forward
with the straightening of the
arm.
• The fencers are now at
straight arm distance to body.

Parries quarte and ripostes.

Parries quarte.

Steps backward and pressures
the blade toward quarte.
• The fencers are now at lunge
distance to body.

Disengages with the counter-
riposte and lunges with the
point to chest, in response.
• An indirect counter-riposte.

(Left-handed/right-handed combination: the opponent's blade is on Fencer B's outside. Fencer B is covered. Fencer A moves hand a little toward quarte, then parries sixte and ripostes. Steps backward and pressures the blade toward sixte.)

8	In sixte.	In sixte.
	Lightly pressures the blade by moving the hand a little toward sixte.	Disengages and lunges to chest.
	Parries quarte.	Recovers backward to sixte. • The distance between the fencers is lunge distance to body.
	Ripostes with a lunge.	Parries quarte and counter-ripostes to chest.

(Left-handed/right-handed combination: the opponent's blade is on Fencer B's outside. Fencer B is covered. Fencer A moves hand a little toward quarte, then parries sixte and ripostes.)

Try this as a choice reaction exercise.

9	In sixte.	In sixte.
	Lightly pressures the blade by moving the hand a little toward sixte.	Disengages and lunges to chest.
	Parries quarte.	Recovers backward to sixte. • The distance between the fencers is lunge distance to body.
	Ripostes with a lunge.	Parries quarte and counter-ripostes direct, or indirect, disengaging with the riposte if the opponent attempts to parry quarte again.

(Left-handed/right-handed combination: the opponent's blade is on Fencer B's outside. Fencer B is covered. Fencer A moves hand a little toward quarte, parries sixte, then ripostes with a lunge. Occasionally attempts to parry sixte again.)

10 In sixte.

In sixte.

Lightly pressures the blade by moving the hand a little toward sixte.

Disengages and lunges to chest.

Parries quarte.

Recovers backward to sixte. The distance between the fencers is lunge distance to body.

Ripostes with a lunge.

Parries counter-sixte and counter-ripostes with opposition, holding on to the blade.

(Left-handed/right-handed combination: the opponent's blade is on Fencer B's outside. Fencer B is covered. Fencer A moves hand a little toward quarte, parries sixte, then ripostes with a lunge.

11 In sixte.

In sixte.

Lightly pressures the blade by moving the hand a little toward sixte.

Disengages with short lunge.

Parries quarte.

Recovers forward.
• The distance between the fencers is straight arm distance to body.

Ripostes.

Parries quarte and counter-riposte to chest.

(Left-handed/right-handed combination: the opponent's blade is on Fencer B's outside. Fencer B is covered. Fencer A moves hand a little toward quarte, parries sixte, then ripostes.)

PART TWO
Sabre

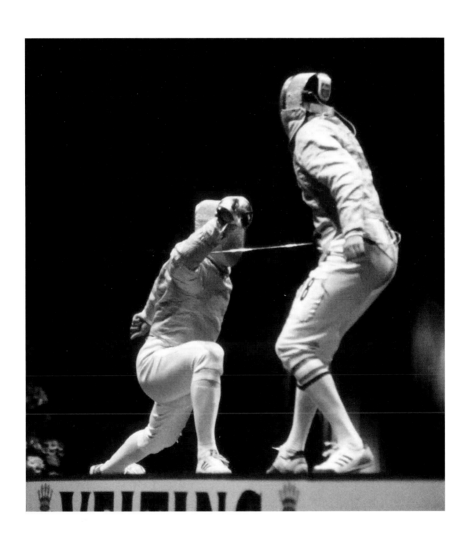

CHAPTER FOUR

Sabre Training

Introduction

The sabre is the modern version of the cavalry sword. The valid target at this weapon is above the waist including the head and arms. The blade is similar in length and weight to the foil. Hits are scored with the point or the cutting edges of the blade. Fencers wear metallic jackets and masks with metallic covering which are connected to the jacket by a wire. This allows hits to be registered by electronic scoring apparatus. The unarmed hand extends below the cuff of the jacket and is not part of the circuit. Similarly, the valid target on the sword arm stops at the cuff. A light touch on the jacket or mask registers a coloured light. No light is registered for off target. A hit off target does not stop the fencing phrase. Sabre is a conventional weapon. Like foil, the first person to attack has right of way. The referee plays an important role by deciding who receives the scored hit.

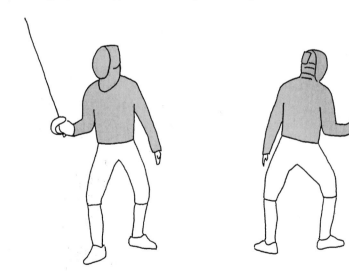

The sabre target.

It is possible to fence without electronic recording apparatus by using judges (at all three weapons). The fencers stand on the piste, with the referee and judges on the sidelines. Two judges stand behind and on either side of each combatant (four judges in total), with the referee between the two fencers at the side of the piste. The judges lift their arms if they see hits on or off target on the opposing fencer. Each judge has one vote and the referee one and a half. Judges can say that a hit has landed, has missed, or can abstain. Two judges that agree (two votes) overrule the referee. Similarly, a referee's decision (one and a half votes) overrules a single judge, if the other judge abstains. The referee decides the phrasing. In a bout where the first to get five hits wins, the fencers will change ends after tree hits, which helps to even out any inconsistencies in the judging. With a left-handed/right-handed combination the fencers come on guard with their sword arms away from the referee (chests facing), so that the hits are easier for the referee to spot. After three hits, the judges change ends.

Using judges to record.

On Guard and Footwork

The on-guard position in sabre is similar to foil, but the shoulders and trunk are turned a little more toward the opponent. The weapon arm is placed a little closer to the trunk than in foil, but still kept clear of the hip. The shoulder should remain entirely relaxed. The point of the blade is on front of the hand at about 45 degrees. The cutting edge and guard face forward and the hand is positioned slightly below the elbow. The principles employed here are that the fencer gives no early indication of an intention to attack and, if attacked, can readily defend. This can be referred to as the offensive–defensive position. For ease of reference, we will simply refer to this as the on-guard position. Sabreurs fence toe to toe.

The defensive box is often characterized by a two-dimensional shape formed by the defensive positions of tierce, quarte and quinte, which form its sides. The true defensive box takes the form of a pyramid on its side, with the top removed. As the defender's hand moves forward, the area being defended reduces.

Because of the fencing measure, sabre is fenced with almost total absence of. blade. This is the distance at which you can hit the opponent's sword arm with a lunge. There is no flèche at sabre. Whilst a crossover (moving one leg over the other) movement of the feet as you move forward is not allowed, it is allowed when you are moving backward. Other than this, footwork in sabre is the same as for foil and tends to be explosive. The lunge is similar.

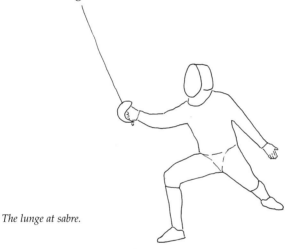

The lunge at sabre.

There are five guards at sabre, which are as follows:

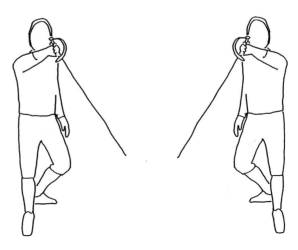

Prime.

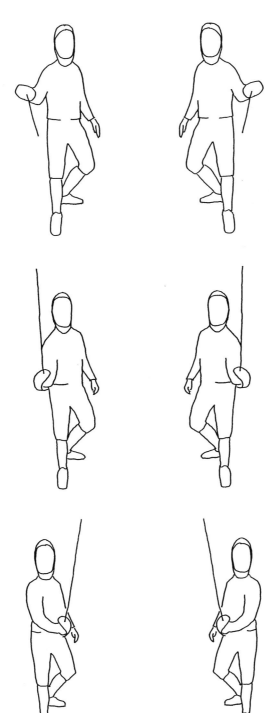

Seconde.

Tierce.

Quarte.

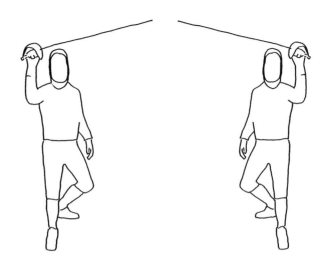

Quinte.

Control of the Weapon

Grip the handle 10mm behind the guard, the thumb on top and the first phalanx of the index finger at the bottom. Allow the other fingers to bend freely around the handle. The little finger holds it against the heel of the hand. Hold the weapon in a relaxed manner. Holding too firmly can cause tiredness in the hand and can result in stiffness in the fingers, the muscles of the hand and shoulder. The grip can be firm or loose, depending on the fencing action employed. The top of the guard of the weapon is slightly extended over the knuckles, which means that right- and left-handed guards are different.

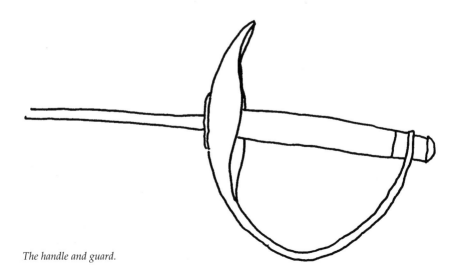

The handle and guard.

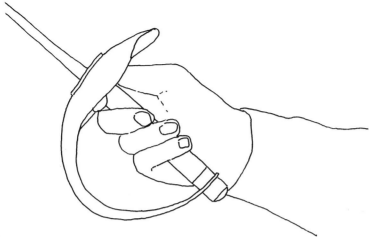

The grip.

A cut may begin with a rotation of the hand to place the fore- or back-edge of the blade in the direction of the opponent's target, the blade travelling the shortest possible route. The arm should straighten without locking the elbow, remaining loose. The cut is delivered with a pushing and pulling action of the thumb and little finger, done concurrently with a firm forward movement of the wrist. The through cut is made with a circular motion (usually to the chest). It is made solely from the wrist and delivered with the last 20mm of the blade. A cut beginning at the chest is drawn through to the flank without swinging the sword arm. The point may also be used to deliver hits, usually with the guard turned in the seconde position (hand pronated).

Come on guard at a distance where you can cut to head by straightening your arm. All these cuts should be made with the last 20–40mm of the blade. For the cut to head the blade is 100–120mm above the mask.

The cut to outside cheek is the right cheek and the cut to inside cheek is the left cheek, for a right-handed opponent. This situation is mirrored for a left-handed opponent (that is, the cut to outside cheek is the left cheek and the cut to inside cheek is the right cheek).

Fencer A	**Fencer B**
In the on-guard position. Gives agreed signal for the training sequence to begin.	In the on-guard position. Straightens the sword arm, cuts crisply to head (leaves arm out), rotates hand and cuts to outside cheek, rotates hand and cuts to head, rotates hand and cuts to outside cheek, and so on.

• Rotate the hand to each line in turn.
• Keep the arm straight and relaxed, positioned directly behind the guard.
• Apply the cuts using the fingers.

Gives agreed signal for the training sequence to end.	Returns to the on-guard position.

Simple Attacks

The simple attack, direct or indirect, is correctly executed when the straightening of the arm, the point or cut threatening the valid target, proceeds the initiation of the lunge. Direct simple attacks take the straightest route to the sabre valid target. Indirect simple attacks comprise one blade movement that passes over or under the opposing blade, bringing about a change in line or returning to the original line. In sabre, simple attacks can be delivered with the point, cut or through cut. Cuts can be delivered with the fore-edge of the blade, or the first third of the back-edge nearest the point, or with the side of the blade (through cut).

To practise simple attacks, start at a distance where you can land a cut to head or flank by straightening your arm. After successful repetition, increase the distance to a lunge. Try to make the cut neat and crisp. Move slowly, then gradually speed up. When you lunge, the hand must move before the foot. Always try to ensure that the cut lands fractionally ahead of the front foot landing. If the front foot lands ahead of the hit, then this can be termed a remise (a renewal of the attack in the same line). The attack ends when the front foot lands.

Come on guard at a distance where you can just cut at your opponent's head by straightening your arm.

Fencer A	**Fencer B**
1 In quinte. Lowers the blade from quinte to seconde.	In the on-guard position. Cuts to head. •Fencer B is cutting into an opening line.
Gives agreed signal for the training sequence to end.	Returns to the on-guard position.

2 In seconde. Raises the blade from seconde to quinte.	In the on-guard position. Cuts to flank. • Fencer B is cutting into an opening line.
Gives agreed signal for the training sequence to end.	Returns to the on-guard position.

(Left-handed/right-handed combination: Fencer B cuts to chest instead of to flank.)

Now increase the distance to lunge distance for a cut to head. When concluding, return backward to guard, returning to the on-guard position.

Typical cuts to head, chest and flank are shown in the illustrations that follow, as well as the application of the point to chest.

A cut to head.

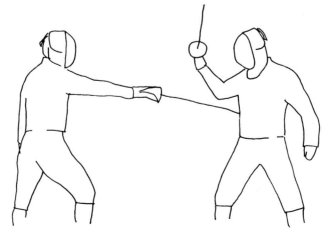

A cut to flank.

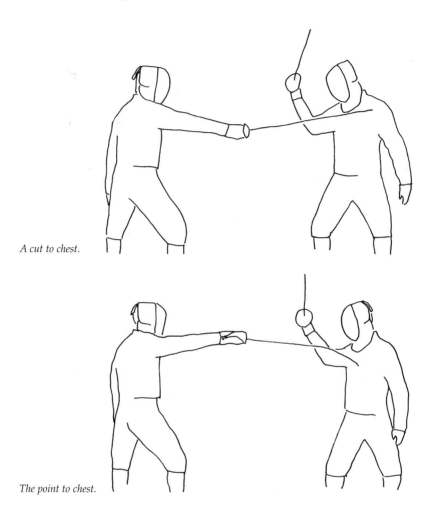

A cut to chest.

The point to chest.

Parries and Ripostes

The parry is a defensive action made with the blade to prevent the attack from landing. This is a protective displacement of the blade that covers exposed target areas, travelling the shortest route between defensive positions. The principle of defence is the opposition of forte to foible. A parry and riposte should be thought of as a single unit. Defence in sabre can be very difficult because of the variety of cuts and the use of the point, combined with the size of the defensive box to be defended. In order to parry successfully, the fencer has either to anticipate the final line of the opponent's attack, or develop very fast reactions. Parries should be taken as late as possible. The position of the attacker's guard toward the end of an attacking sequence may give some indication.

Parries are split into two groups:

- the first defensive triangle: prime; seconde; quinte
- the second defensive triangle: tierce; quarte; quinte.

The riposte is the offensive action made by the fencer who has success-fully parried the attack. This can be direct, indirect or compound and delivered immediately or after a delay, the fencer responding to the light-est touch of the attacker's blade. The response can be made with a cut, through cut, or the point.

The second defensive triangle is a useful place to start. Maintain each of these defensive positions until the blade is touched. Ensure that all the parries are formed correctly. Wait for your opponent's blade to meet yours, then riposte crisply, the cuts executed lightly using the fingers. Begin the parry of quarte by first turning the guard.

Direct ripostes take the most direct route to the target. Following are some examples.

Start on guard at lunge distance to head or body.

Fencer A	**Fencer B**
1 In the on-guard position. Lunges with a cut to chest. Stays on the lunge.	In the on-guard position. Parries quarte and ripostes with a cut to head.
Recovers backward to the on-guard position. Leaves the arm straight until the front foot has landed, then bends the sword arm.	Returns to the on-guard position.
2 In the on-guard position. Lunges with a cut to flank. Stays on the lunge.	In the on-guard position. Parries tierce and ripostes with a cut to head.
Recovers backward to the on-guard position.	Returns to the on-guard position.
3 In the on-guard position. Lunges with a cut to head. Stays on the lunge.	In the on-guard position. Parries quinte and ripostes with a cut to flank.
Recovers backward to the on-guard position.	Returns to the on-guard position.

(Left-handed/right-handed com1bination: in 3., Fencer B parries quinte and ripostes with a cut to chest.)

A high parry of quarte can also be used in sabre as an alternative to quinte, particularly with the left-handed/right-handed combination.

Indirect ripostes consist of one blade action, which passes over or under the attacker's blade, on its way to the target. Here are some examples.

Start on guard at lunge distance to head or body.

Fencer A	**Fencer B**
1 In the on-guard position. Lunges with a cut to chest. Stays on the lunge.	In the on-guard position. Parries quarte.
Parries quinte, anticipating. Still on the lunge.	Ripostes with a cut to flank, hitting into the opening line.
Recovers backward to the on-guard position.	Returns to the on-guard position.

(Left-handed/right-handed combination: Fencer B ripostes with a cut to chest.)

2 In the on-guard position. Lunges with a cut to flank. Stays on the lunge.	In the on-guard position. Parries tierce.
Parries quinte, anticipating. Still on the lunge. Recovers backward to the on-guard position.	Ripostes with a cut to chest, hitting into the opening line. Returns to the on-guard position.

(Left-handed/right-handed combination: Fencer B ripostes with a cut to flank.)

3 In the on-guard position. Lunges with a cut to head. Stays on the lunge.	In the on-guard position. Parries quinte.
Parries tierce, anticipating. Still on the lunge.	Ripostes with a cut to head, hitting into the opening line.
Recovers backward to the on-guard position.	Returns to the on-guard position.

Having mastered all of these parries and ripostes, Fencer A now immediately recovers to guard following Fencer B's parry; Fencer B will lunge with the riposte. Repeat the previous two exercises incorporating the lunge. Fencer A can then vary his attacks and Fencer B will have to select the correct responses, with and without the lunge.

Counter-Ripostes

A counter-riposte is an offensive action, which follows the successful parry of a riposte or counter-riposte. It can be simple, or compound and delivered by the attacker or the defender. It is an action of second intention.

Start by doing three parries and ripostes in succession. After this routine has been established, introduce the counter-ripostes. Concentrate on technique; speed will come later. The cut to flank is a horizontal cut, with the hand in pronation. Start at a distance where a cut to head can land by straightening your arm (no lunge). Try to maintain a rhythm. The three actions should follow in turn with no pause between the parries and ripostes.

Stand on guard at straight arm distance to head. The exercise begins with three parries and ripostes, correctly executed. When mastered, the counter-ripostes can be introduced gradually as the next development.

Fencer A	Fencer B
1 In the on-guard position. Cuts to chest.	In the on-guard position. Parries quarte and ripostes with a cut to head.
Cuts to flank.	Parries tierce and ripostes with a cut to head.
Cuts to head.	Parries quinte and ripostes with a cut to head.
Gives agreed signal for the training sequence to end.	Returns to the on-guard position.

Next, the counter-ripostes are introduced into the sequence. Fencer A does not have to parry every counter-riposte.

2   In the on-guard position.
Cuts to chest.

In the on-guard position.
Parries quarte and ripostes with
a cut to head.
* Begin slowly but rhythmically,
   gradually speeding up, but
   maintaining the rhythm at all
   times.

Parries quinte and counter-
ripostes with a cut to flank.
• Whilst okay as an elementary
   training sequence, a parry of
   quinte is difficult to sustain at
   an advanced level against a
   parry of quarte and fast
   riposte to head.

Parries tierce and counter-
ripostes with a cut to head.

Parries quinte and counter-
ripostes with a cut to head.

Parries quinte and counter-
ripostes with a cut to head.

Gives agreed signal for the
training sequence to end.

Returns to the on-guard position.

(Left-handed/right-handed combination: whilst okay as an elementary
training sequence, a parry of quinte is difficult to sustain at an advanced
level against a parry of tierce and fast counter-riposte to head.)

Compound Attacks

A compound attack comprises one or more feints. To be successful, a feint
must be sufficiently deep (realistic), in order to draw the parry. First, practise the hand movements at close quarters, then try a deep straight thrust
with cut to head (for depth). Now practise the compound attack with a
deep feint to head, the hand rotating during the lunge (progressively). Try
to get the hit to land at the latest when the front foot lands (see illustra-
tion on opposite page).

Start at a distance where you can land a cut to head or flank by straightening your arm. Close quarter work like this will help to keep Fencer B's
hand in place when rotating. Fencer A moves from quinte to seconde and
back again. This particular opening helps to keep the forward elbow out
of harm's way when the cut to flank is attempted. If the cuts are delivered
too heavily then change them to two little double cuts, delivered in quick
succession.

A compound attack, finishing to chest.

Fencer A

In quinte.
Moves hand from quinte to seconde, offering an opening for a
head cut.

Moves hand from seconde to
quinte, offering an opening for
a flank cut.

Steps backward, moves hand
from quinte to seconde.
• The fencers are now at lunge
distance for a cut to head.

Moves hand from seconde to
quinte.

Starts to steps forward, moves
hand from quinte to seconde.

Fencer B

In the on-guard position.
Lightly cuts to head and leaves
the blade out.
• Try not to overstretch and
keep the arm relaxed.

Lightly cuts to flank by rotating
hand, leaving the blade out.
• Fencer B should not touch the
blade.

Lunges, lightly cuts to head
and leaves the blade out.
Stays on the lunge.

Lightly cuts to flank by rotating
the hand
Is still on the lunge.
Prepares to recover backward.

Recovers backward immediately, keeping the sword arm
straight. Lightly cuts to head by

Fencer A	Fencer B
	rotating the hand. The cut lands as Fencer A completes the step. • The fencers are now at straight arm distance for a cut to head.
Moves hand from seconde to quinte.	Lightly cuts to flank by rotating hand, leaving the blade out.
Moves hand from quinte to seconde.	Lightly cuts to head by rotating hand, leaving the blade out.
Steps backward, moves hand from seconde to quinte. • The fencers are now at lunge distance for a cut to head.	Lunges, lightly cuts to flank and leaves the blade out. Stays on the lunge.
And so on.	
Gives agreed signal for the training sequence to end.	Returns to the on-guard position.

Gradually speed up and make the actions more progressive. (Left-handed/right-handed combination: Fencer B can cut to chest instead of to flank.)

Next, try this at lunge distance to head.

Fencer A	**Fencer B**
1 In quinte. Moves hand from quinte to seconde, offering an opening for a head cut.	In the on-guard position. Lunges and lightly cuts to head with a simple attack, hitting before the front foot lands, then recovers backward to guard.

The simple attack is deep and effective. Fencer A now has a reason to parry, which leads to the compound attack.

Fencer A	**Fencer B**
2 In quinte. Moves hand from quinte to seconde.	In the on-guard position. Lunges this time with a feint to head.

Fencer A	Fencer B
Moves hand from seconde to quinte during the course of the lunge.	Rotates the hand progressively during lunge, lightly cuts to flank before the front foot lands, then recovers backward to guard.

Next, begin with a cut to flank.

Fencer A	**Fencer B**
1 In seconde. Moves hand from seconde to quinte, offering an opening for a flank cut.	In the on-guard position. Lunges and lightly cuts to flank, moving the hand directly to the horizontal flank cut position, hitting before the front foot lands, then recovers backward to guard.
2 In seconde. Moves hand from seconde to quinte.	In the on-guard position. Lunges this time with a feint to flank.
Moves hand from quinte to seconde during the course of the lunge.	Rotates the hand progressively during lunge, lightly cuts to head before the front foot lands, then recovers backward to guard.

(Left-handed/right-handed combination: Fencer B may wish to try cuts to chest instead of to flank.)

Next, try the same compound attacks at step and lunge distance to head or flank. Make the first step small. Do a short, well-balanced lunge. At this stage, accuracy is more important than speed. Recover to guard then step backward to resume the correct distance.

Successive Parries and Ripostes

Successive parries are consecutive parries that respond to a compound attack, whose ultimate aim is to find the attacking blade. The parries are timed according to the speed of the attacking actions. The final parry should be taken as late as possible and not all feints should be reacted to. Start at lunge distance to head, chest or flank.

Begin with a parry and riposte.

Fencer A	**Fencer B**
1 In the on-guard position. Lunges with a cut to flank.	In the on-guard position. Parries tierce and ripostes immediately with a cut to head.
Recovers backward to guard.	Returns to guard.

Next, Fencer A introduces the compound attack. Fencer B responds with successive parries.

Fencer A	**Fencer B**
2 In the on-guard position. Lunges with a feint to flank.	In the on-guard position. Begins to parry tierce.
Rotates the hand progressively during lunge and attempts to cut to chest.	Parries quarte and ripostes immediately with a cut to head.
Recovers backward to guard.	Returns to guard.

Again, begin with a parry and riposte.

Fencer A	**Fencer B**
1 In the on-guard position. Lunges with a cut to head.	In the on-guard position. Parries quinte and ripostes immediately with a cut to head.
Recovers backward to guard.	Returns to guard.

Next, Fencer A introduces the compound attack. Fencer B responds with successive parries.

Fencer A	**Fencer B**
2 In the on-guard position. Lunges with feint to head.	In the on-guard position. Begins to parry quinte.
Rotates the hand progressively during lunge and attempts to cut to flank.	Parries seconde and ripostes immediately with a cut to head.

Recovers backward to guard.   Returns to guard.

Preparations

A preparation of attack is any movement that prepares the way. This can be a movement of feet, blade or both. The end results can be simple or compound. A list of typical preparations is included in Chapter 1 on foil training. Two common preparations in sabre are the step forward and the beat attack.

First, ensure that you are at full sabre fencing measure. When you train, you should just be able to cut to wrist when you lunge. To cut to head, chest or flank will require a step and lunge.

Fencer A	**Fencer B**
1 In quinte. Moves hand from quinte to seconde.	In the on-guard position. Takes a small step forward, straightening the sword arm with the landing of the rear foot and lunges with a cut to head.
Returns to guard as Fencer B recovers.	Recovers backward with sword arm still straight, steps backward, then resumes guard. • Do not bend the sword arm until the previous distance is resumed.
2 In seconde. Moves hand from seconde to quinte.	In the on-guard position. Takes a small step forward, straightening the sword arm with the landing of the rear foot (rotating the hand at the same time) and lunges with a cut to flank.
Returns to guard as Fencer B recovers.	Recovers backward with sword arm still straight, steps backward, then resumes guard. • Do not bend the sword arm until the previous distance is resumed.

(Left-handed/right-handed combination: Fencer B may wish to cut to chest instead of to flank.)

Fencer A now alternates the last two exercises randomly and at different speeds.

A beat is distinctly different from an engagement. With an engagement to quarte the hand moves across to the quarte position. With the beat the hand stays on the tierce side, performing a short offensive action on the opponent's blade, by using the fingers. If it is too wide it can be deceived. When training, the attacker should beat the centre of the blade. Sabre beats will typically be executed with a step forward, beating when the rear foot lands, followed immediately by a lunge. They can be made with the fore-edge of the blade, either downward or across, and also with the back-edge. It must be delivered on the top two-thirds of the defender's blade.

Start by practising with the hand close enough to strike the centre of the opponent's blade with a slight extension of the arm. The beat should typically be 175mm wide, which is difficult to deceive.

Next, go to lunge distance for a cut to head.

Fencer A	**Fencer B**
1 In seconde. Raises the hand from seconde and extends the sword arm with the point in line.	In the on-guard position. Beats the side of the opponent's blade and lunges with a cut to head. • Ensure that the hand moves forward ahead of the foot when lunging to head.
Returns to guard.	Recovers backward to guard.

Then try step and lunge distance to head.

Fencer A	**Fencer B**
2 In seconde. Raises the hand from seconde and extends the sword arm with the point in line.	In the on-guard position. Takes a small step forward, executing the beat with the landing of the rear foot, and lunges with a cut to head. • Ensure that the hand moves forward ahead of the foot when lunging to head.
Returns to guard.	Recovers backward with sword arm still straight, steps back-

ward, then resumes guard.
- Do not bend the sword arm until the previous distance is resumed.

Then go back to lunge distance for a cut to head.

Fencer A	Fencer B
1 In the on-guard position. Gives agreed signal for the training sequence to begin.	In the on-guard position. Executes beat this time with the back-edge of the blade and lunges with a cut to outside cheek. • The beat takes place between the opponent's blade and mask, with an immediate result..
Still in the on-guard position.	Recovers backward to guard.

The cut to outside cheek is the right cheek for a right-handed opponent. This situation is mirrored for a left-handed opponent (that is, the cut to outside cheek is the left cheek).

Next try step and lunge distance to head.

Fencer A	Fencer B
2 In the on-guard position. Gives agreed signal for the training sequence to begin.	In the on-guard position. Takes a small step forward, executing the beat with the back-edge of the blade with the landing of the rear foot, and lunges with a cut to outside cheek.
Still in the on-guard position.	Recovers backward with sword arm still straight, steps backward, then resumes guard.

(Left-handed/right-handed combination: in 1. and 2., Fencer B cuts to inside cheek rather than outside.)

Counter-Attacks

This is an offensive action delivered on the opponent's attack in such a way that it gains a period of fencing time on it and arrests it. A period of fencing time might be the time taken to do a parry or to take a step. A typical counter-attack at sabre is the stop-cut.

Begin at straight arm distance to the extended target and wear a training sleeve. Try not to touch the guard. Aim to hit cleanly on the wrist. If the hits land further up the arm then you are too close.

Begin with stop-cuts.

Fencer A	**Fencer B**
1 In the on-guard position. Begins attack to chest by straightening the sword arm, with the wrist exposed.	In the on-guard position. Stop-cuts wrist with the upper front-edge of the blade.
Returns to guard.	Returns to guard.
2 In the on-guard position. Begins attack to flank by straightening the sword arm, with the wrist exposed.	In the on-guard position. Stop-cuts wrist with the upper front-edge of the blade.
Returns to guard.	Returns to guard.
3 In the on-guard position. Begins attack to head by straightening the sword arm, with underside of the wrist exposed.	In the on-guard position. Stop-cuts under wrist with the upper front-edge of the blade (or upper back-edge).
Returns to guard.	Returns to guard.

Next, we can introduce a parry and riposte. The stop-cut may not land successfully, after all.

Fencer A	**Fencer B**
1 In the on-guard position. Begins attack to chest by straightening the sword arm, with the wrist exposed.	In the on-guard position. Stop-cuts wrist with the upper front-edge of the blade, parries quarte and ripostes with a cut to head.

	Returns to guard.	Returns to guard.
2	In the on-guard position. Begins attack to flank by straightening the sword arm, with the wrist exposed.	In the on-guard position. Stop-cuts wrist with the upper front-edge of the blade, parries tierce and ripostes with a cut to head.
	Returns to guard.	Returns to guard.
3	In the on-guard position. Begins attack to head by straightening the sword arm, with underside of the wrist exposed.	In the on-guard position. Stop-cuts under wrist with the upper front-edge of the blade (or upper back-edge), parries quinte and ripostes with a cut to head.
	Returns to guard.	Returns to guard.

Now do the last three exercises in quick succession. Join them up without stopping. After the three actions you can have a little pause, then start again.

Next, Fencer B will add a small step backward after the stop-cut. The step backward, like the parry, creates a period of fencing time that places the counter-attack ahead of the attack. Fencer A will continue the attack with a step forward, gradually deepening the attack, which will then be parried and riposted. Fencer B has gained the initiative with the step; the parry and riposte following this is a good safety stroke in case the stop-cut misses.

Do all three actions in quick succession, as before.

Counter-Time

Counter-time is an action made by an attacker on the opponent's attempt to stop-hit or stop-cut, parrying it and riposting. This is an action of second intention. The means by which a stop-cut can be drawn are many. These can be slightly uncovered feints, attacks on the blade which draw a deception, stepping forward, and so on. The success of counter-time is very much in the timing of the parry. If the parry is anticipated or taken too early, then the opponent is free to apply his or her own second intentions.

Begin at step and lunge distance for a cut to head.

Fencer A	**Fencer B**
In the on-guard position. Gives agreed signal for the training sequence to begin.	In the on-guard position. Takes a short step forward and straightens the sword arm with the action of the rear foot.
Stop-cuts with an angulated cut to the wrist, being careful not to touch the guard.	Parries quarte, ripostes to head with lunge. • The key to this operation is the initial short step that leaves time for the parry to take place. • In this position, Fencer B's hand is well forward and the resulting parry is small. • Remember to turn the guard.
Returns to guard as Fencer B recovers.	Recovers backward with sword arm still straight, steps backward, then resumes guard.

(Left-handed/right-handed combination: the angulated cut for Fencer A is likely to elicit a response of tierce.)

CHAPTER FIVE

Advanced Sabre Training

Introduction

Give clear, unambiguous openings and concentrate on economic, precise hand and foot actions that are well co-ordinated. We will assume (unless otherwise stated) that the fencers start from an on-guard position.

Step by lifting toe and heel. Concentrate on keeping balance. For the initial small step forward, the front foot moves slowly, with a fast rear foot. Keep legs bent. Do not allow your weight to move forward or backward. You cannot do a balestra after a small step forward if you are leaning forward. There are two types of balestra: a short one the same length as a step; and a longer one that takes you a little closer to the opponent. To change direction requires good footwork. An opponent will tend to react to the beginning of a step forward. At sabre, it is still acceptable to crossover when stepping backward. A large step backward is required after delivering a stop-cut to wrist. Go back with small steps if you wish your opponent to attack.

Simple and Compound Attacks

A simple attack is an attack into a known line, which must be done from a realistic distance and realistic blade presentation.

Start at close quarters, then lunge distance, then step and lunge distance to head. To get two steps and lunge, Fencer A steps backward immediately in response to Fencer B's first step. When lunging, care must be taken to ensure that the foot does not land ahead of the attacking blade, as this can be termed a remise. With the step and lunge, the first small step is exploratory. If the opponent attacks on the preparation there is time to parry and riposte, or if there is no reaction the attack may continue. These openings should be done with small, delicate hand actions.

Practise these openings at various distances. Drawings showing a coach giving these openings are included in Chapter 6.

Fencer A	**Fencer B**
1 In the on-guard position.	In the on-guard position.

Lowers the blade by rotating the hand a little in pronation.	Lightly cuts to head.
• This has the effect of creating a small opening line to the head.	
Returns to guard	Returns to guard.
Lifts the blade to quinte.	Lightly cuts to flank.
• This has the effect of creating an opening line to the flank.	
Returns to guard.	Returns to guard.
Turns the blade a little back to tierce.	Cuts to chest.
• This has the effect of creating a small opening line to the chest.	
Returns to guard.	Returns to guard.
And so on.	

We will assume that the fencers are now well versed in returning to guard following the successful completion of an exercise and this can be taken as read.

Now vary the order of these three openings as well as varying the distance. At lunge distance, Fencer A can step forward with the opening if you want the other fencer to hit you with a straight arm. At step lunge distance, Fencer A can step forward with the opening if you want the other fencer to hit you with a lunge. If Fencer A steps forward or backward without giving an opening, the other fencer should simply respond by keeping distance.

Try this first at lunge distance, then step and lunge distance to head.

Fencer A	Fencer B
1 In quinte.	In the on-guard position.
Lower the blade a little, then bring it back up.	Cuts to head before blade gets to quinte.
• Fencer A gradually reduces the time available for the cut to land.	

Fencer A	**Fencer B**
2 In quinte. Lower the blade a little, then bring it back up.	In the on-guard position. Attempts to cut to head before blade gets to quinte.
Takes a small step backward and successfully parries the simple attack and ripostes to head.	

The parry is now successful because of the introduction of the small step backward. Now Fencer B needs to introduce a compound attack, say head-flank.

For skills training, practise small head-flank actions around the guard at close quarters. With one fencer in the quinte position, the fencer practising the attack rotates the hand between head and flank without touching the blade or guard and back again. The blade actions should be as small as possible. The flank action can also be done to wrist.

A good head-flank is done progressively. The step is small and slow with the feint to head and accelerates progressively into the cut to flank.

Fencer A	**Fencer B**
1 In the on-guard position. Lowers the blade by rotating the hand a little in pronation.	In the on-guard position. Feints a cut to head, either by straightening the sword arm (at lunge distance to flank), or by stepping forward and straightening the sword arm (at step and lunge distance to flank), and starts to lunge.
Parries quinte, responding late as though to a real attack.	Rotates the hand progressively during course of the lunge and lightly cuts to flank.

Now practise step and lunge distance to head.

Fencer A	**Fencer B**
2 In the on-guard position. Steps forward and lowers the	In the on-guard position. Immediately lunges with a feint

blade by rotating the hand a little in pronation.
• The fencers are now at lunge distance for a cut to head.

cut to head as Fencer A closes the distance.

Parries quinte, reacting.

Rotates the hand progressively during the course of the lunge and lightly cuts to flank.

(Left-handed/right-handed combination: with 1. and 2., cuts to chest instead of to flank.)

Next, try a compound attack with two feints at step and lunge distance to head. In sabre, it is possible to feint into the blade as well as into the open or opening line. Fencer A's little hand movement to quarte is optional.

Fencer A	**Fencer B**
1 In the on-guard position. Opens up a little on the flank side by moving the hand slightly toward quarte.	In the on-guard position. Steps forward and feints directly into blade (toward flank). • The fencers are now at lunge distance to head or flank.
Steps backward, covering flank by moving the hand toward tierce. • The fencers are now at step and lunge distance to head or flank.	Explosive, does a balestra head-flank, accelerating.

(Left-handed/right-handed combination: cuts to chest instead of to flank.)

Lunge distance for a cut to inside cheek or flank. Be careful not to hit the defender's elbow. Start with a simple attack.

Fencer A	**Fencer B**
1 In the on-guard position. Moves the hand to seconde, providing an opening line.	In the on-guard position. Lunges in response with a cut to inside cheek.

The cut to inside cheek is the left cheek, for a right-handed opponent. This situation is mirrored for a left-handed opponent (that is, the cut to inside cheek is the right cheek).

Now proceed to a compound attack.

Fencer A	Fencer B
2 In the on-guard position. Moves the hand to seconde, providing an opening line.	In the on-guard position. Lunges in response with a feint to inside cheek.
Parries quarte. Rotates the hand with a circular motion from seconde until it reaches quarte.	Rotates the hand progressively during course of the lunge and lightly cuts to flank.
3 In the on-guard position. Lowers the blade by rotating the hand a little in pronation.	In the on-guard position. Begins to step forward with a feint to head.
Steps backward immediately, ensuring that lunge distance for a cut to inside cheek or flank is maintained.	Lunges in with a feint to inside cheek and a sudden acceleration of pace.
Parries quarte. Rotates the hand with a circular motion until it reaches quarte.	Rotates the hand progressively during course of the lunge and lightly cuts to flank.

Next, practise lunge distance for a cut to outside cheek or flank. Start with a simple attack.

Fencer A	Fencer B
In seconde. 1 Moves the hand to quinte, providing an opening line.	In the on-guard position. Lunges in response with a cut to flank.

Now proceed to a compound attack.

Fencer A	**Fencer B**
2 In seconde. Moves the hand to quinte, providing an opening line.	In the on-guard position. Lunges in response with a cut to flank.
Parries seconde.	Rotates the hand progressively during course of the lunge and lightly cuts to outside cheek.
3 In the on-guard position. Moves the hand to quinte, providing an opening line.	In the on-guard position. Begins to step forward with feint to flank.
Steps backward immediately, maintaining distance. Parries seconde. • The fencers are once again at lunge distance for a cut to inside cheek.	Rotates the hand progressively during course of the lunge and lightly cuts to outside cheek.

Defence against Simple and Compound Attacks

If an attacker advances, one can retreat for a while in order to maintain distance, but eventually the end of the piste will be reached. Start at step and lunge distance for a cut to head.

Fencer A	**Fencer B**
1 In the on-guard position. Steps forward.	In the on-guard position. Steps backward immediately, maintaining distance.
Steps forward. • The fencers are now at lunge distance for a cut to head, chest or flank.	Either does nothing, or moves hand to tierce or quinte.
Lunges with a cut to head, chest or flank. • A simple attack.	Parries quinte, quarte, or tierce and ripostes with a cut to head.

If the wrist position is exposed on the attacker's step forward, a stop-cut can be introduced. If the attacker steps forward twice, the parry is taken with a step backward.

Fencer A	**Fencer B**
2 In the on-guard position. Steps forward, exposing underneath the wrist a little.	In the on-guard position. Stop-cuts under the wrist and steps backward. • The fencers are now at lunge distance for a cut to head, chest or flank.
Lunges with a cut to head, chest or flank. • A simple attack.	Parries quinte, quarte or tierce and ripostes with a cut to head.

Now we can alternate these two openings randomly, occasionally introducing a counter-riposte sequence. Learning to present and read these two openings is a real test of skill. Maintain distance and add movement. The attacker finishes in different lines.

For successive parries (the defence against a compound attack), the approach is similar to the defence against a simple attack. Step and lunge distance for a cut to head.

Fencer A	**Fencer B**
1 In the on-guard position. Takes a small step forward.	In the on-guard position. Steps backward, maintaining distance.
Takes a large step forward. • The fencers are now at short lunge distance to chest or flank. Begins to lunge with a feint cut to chest.	Turns the guard early into quarte. • This ensures that the attacker's hand rotates early.
Rotates the hand progressively during the course of the lunge and lightly cuts to flank.	Steps a little backward. • The fencers are now at long lunge distance to flank. Parries tierce and ripostes with a cut to head.

The late parry paves the way for a broken-time attack.

Fencer A	**Fencer B**
2 In the on-guard position. Takes a step forward. • The fencers are now at lunge distance to chest or flank. Begins to lunge with a feint cut to chest.	In the on-guard position. Turns the guard early into quarte.
Pulls hand back during the course of the lunge as the front foot lands.	Parries tierce, anticipating a final line to flank.
Cuts to chest, hitting into the opening line. • This action requires an element of surprise.	

Then, an appropriate response:

Fencer A	**Fencer B**
3 In the on-guard position. Takes a step forward. • The fencers are now at lunge distance to chest or flank. Begins to lunge with a feint cut to chest.	In the on-guard position. Turns the guard early into quarte.
Pulls hand back during the course of the lunge as the front foot lands.	Stop-cuts to wrist. • The element of surprise has been lost.

Simple and Compound Ripostes

Like simple attacks, simple ripostes can be direct or indirect. One of the commonest indirect ripostes is the parry of quinte followed by a riposte with cut to head. Compound ripostes comprise one or more feints.

Start at step and lunge distance for a cut to head for the next three exercises.

Fencer A	**Fencer B**
1 In the on-guard position. Steps forward and lunges with a cut to head, stays on the lunge.	In the on-guard position. Parries quinte and ripostes with a cut to head (indirect).
2 In the on-guard position. Steps forward and lunges with a cut to head.	In the on-guard position. Parries quinte and ripostes with a feint cut to head.
Recovers backward from the lunge and parries quinte, anticipating.	Rotates hand, without touching the blade and lunges with a cut to flank.

(Left-handed/right-handed combination: with 2., Fencer B may finish with a cut to chest.)

Fencer A	**Fencer B**
1 In the on-guard position. Steps forward and lunges with a cut to chest, stays on the lunge.	In the on-guard position. Parries quarte and ripostes with a cut to flank (indirect).

(Left-handed/right-handed combination: Fencer B ripostes with a cut to chest.)

2 In the on-guard position. Steps forward and lunges with a cut to chest.	In the on-guard position. Parries quarte and ripostes with a feint cut to flank.
Recovers backward from the lunge and parries tierce, anticipating.	Rotates hand, without touching the blade and lunges with a cut to chest.

(Left-handed/right-handed combination: Fencer B ripostes with a feint cut to chest, rotates hand and lunges with a cut to flank.)

Fencer A	Fencer B
1 In the on-guard position. Steps forward and lunges with a cut to flank, stays on the lunge.	In the on-guard position. Parries tierce and ripostes with a cut to chest (indirect).

(Left-handed/right-handed combination: Fencer B parries tierce and ripostes with a cut to flank.)

Fencer A	Fencer B
2 In the on-guard position. Steps forward and lunges with a cut to flank.	In the on-guard position. Parries tierce and ripostes with a feint cut to chest.
Recovers backward from the lunge and parries quarte, anticipating.	Rotates hand, without touching the blade and lunges with a cut to flank.

(Left-handed/right-handed combination: Fencer B parries tierce and ripostes with a feint cut to flank. Fencer A parries tierce, anticipating. Fencer B rotates hand and lunges with a cut to chest.)

Practise these three exercises again, but this time with Fencer A varying the timing. This is now a timing exercise.

Simple and Compound Counter-Ripostes

These can be premeditated (second intention), or reactive. Take the counter parry from a straight arm, with the hand position well forward in the parry. Avoid the use of quarte-head during the sequence, as this can be very hard to parry.
    Start at lunge distance for a cut to head.

Fencer A	Fencer B
In the on-guard position.	In the on-guard position.
1 Lowers the blade by rotating the hand a little in pronation.	Lunges with a cut to head.
Parries quinte and ripostes with a cut to head.	Parries quinte still on the lunge, immediately ripostes with a cut to flank.

> • The hand moves from the straight arm position to the parry, which is taken well forward.

(Left-handed/right-handed combination: Fencer B ripostes with a cut to chest.)

Fencer A	**Fencer B**

2   In the on-guard position. Lowers the blade by rotating the hand a little in pronation.

In the on-guard position. Lunges with a cut to head.

Parries quinte and begins to riposte.

Recovers backward with the arm still straight.
• The fencers are once again at lunge distance for a cut to head.

Lunges with a cut to head

Parries quinte and immediately ripostes with a cut to head.

3   In the on-guard position. Lowers the blade by rotating the hand a little in pronation.

In the on-guard position. Lunges with a cut to head.

Parries quinte and begins to riposte.

Recovers backward with the arm still straight.
• The fencers are once again at lunge distance for a cut to head.

Lunges with a cut to head

Parries quinte and ripostes with a feint cut to head.

Parries quinte, still on the lunge.

Rotates hand with a cut to flank.

(Left-handed/right-handed combination: Fencer B rotates hand with a cut to flank.)

This time, Fencer A starts in quarte, at lunge distance for a cut to chest.

Fencer A	**Fencer B**
1 In the on-guard position. Moves hand to tierce.	In the on-guard position. Lunges with a cut to chest, attacking into the opening line.
Parries quarte and ripostes with a cut to chest.	Parries quarte still on the lunge and immediately ripostes with a cut to head. • The hand moves from the straight arm position to the parry, staying well forward.
2 In the on-guard position. Moves hand to tierce.	In the on-guard position. Lunges with a cut to chest, attacking into the opening line.
Parries quarte and begins to riposte.	Recovers backward with the arm still straight. • The fencers are once again at lunge distance for a cut to head.
Lunges with a cut to chest.	Parries quarte and immediately ripostes with a cut to head.
3 In the on-guard position. Moves hand to tierce.	In the on-guard position. Lunges with a cut to chest, attacking into the opening line.
Parries quarte and begins to riposte.	Recovers backward with the arm still straight. • The fencers are once again at lunge distance for a cut to head.
Lunges with a cut to chest.	Parries quarte and ripostes with a feint cut to head.
Parries quinte, still on the lunge.	Rotates hand with a cut to flank.

(Left-handed/right-handed combination: Fencer B finishes with a cut to chest.)

Preparations

The commonest blade preparation in sabre is a beat, which can be done after a step forward, step backward, or with a sudden change in direction. Beats are attacks au fer (attacks on the blade), while an engagement is an elementary form of prise de fer (taking the blade). Always remember that you do not need to beat the blade in sabre and foil if you already have priority, because these are conventional weapons. If the line is out, this can be cleared using the beat, which is performed with the fingers and the wrist, not by moving the hand. Some additional routines on the use of preparations are included in Chapter 6.

Start at step and lunge distance for a cut to head. Start with an attack to the head.

Fencer A	**Fencer B**
1 In the on-guard position. Lowers the blade by rotating the hand a little in pronation, then extends the sword arm after Fencer B has launched the attack. • Both hits land.	In the on-guard position. Steps forward and lunges with a cut to head. • Fencer B has priority.
2 In the on-guard position. Extends the point in line with the opponent's target.	In the on-guard position. Steps forward and beats the blade with the landing of the back foot and lunges with a cut to head. • Fencer B has regained priority.

Now mix both options randomly so that Fencer B has to choose the correct response (choice reaction). Substitute a balestra instead of the step to give an explosive ending.

A beat can be done to get a reaction. The following routine starts at lunge distance for a cut to head or flank.

Fencer A	**Fencer B**
1 In the on-guard position. Extends the point in line with the opponent's target.	In the on-guard position. Beats the blade and begins to lunge.

Reacts by going to quinte.	Rotates hand, without touching the blade and lunges with a cut to flank.

(Left-handed/right-handed combination: Fencer B lunges with a cut to chest.)

Next, an engagement; step and lunge distance for a cut to head.

Fencer A	**Fencer B**
In the on-guard position. Gives agreed signal for the training sequence to begin.	In the on-guard position. Takes a small step forward, lightly engages the blade in quarte (synchronizing the engagement with the landing of the rear foot). • If deceived, Fencer B can parry and riposte (by turning the guard, with the hand well forward) and lunge with a cut to head.

In sabre, the first step forward is a small exploratory step. What follows next could be another step forward, lunge or a step backward. Step and lunge distance to head.

	Fencer A	**Fencer B**
1	In the on-guard position. Lowers the blade by rotating the hand a little in pronation.	In the on-guard position. Steps forward and lunges with a cut to head; the rear foot moves faster than the front foot, accelerating into the lunge.
2	In the on-guard position. Lowers the blade by rotating the hand a little in pronation.	In the on-guard position. Steps forward.
	Moves backward as the attacker steps forward, in response.	Steps forward and lunges with a cut to head.
3	In the on-guard position.	In the on-guard position.

Lowers the blade by rotating the hand a little in pronation.	Steps forward.
Moves backward as the attacker steps forward, in response.	Does balestra and lunges with a cut to head.

4	In the on-guard position. Lowers the blade by rotating the hand a little in pronation.	In the on-guard position. Steps forward.
	Moves backward as the attacker steps forward. Anticipates by parrying quinte, expecting the opponent to finish with an attack to head, as previously.	Does a balestra and lunges with a cut to flank.

(Left-handed/right-handed combination: Fencer B lunges with a cut to chest.)

Attacks on the Preparation

Step and lunge distance for a cut to head:

Fencer A	**Fencer B**

1	In the on-guard position. Gives agreed signal for the training sequence to begin.	In the on-guard position. Takes a small step forward, then a small step backward.
	Steps forward, following. • The fencers are now at lunge distance for a cut to head.	Lunges immediately with a cut to head, attacking into the preparation.

If Fencer A parries quinte, Fencer B can do a compound attack on the preparation.

2	In the on-guard position. Gives agreed signal for the training sequence to begin.	In the on-guard position. Takes a small step forward, then a small step backward.
	Steps forward, following. • The fencers are now at lunge distance for a cut to head.	Lunges immediately with a feint cut to head.

Parries quinte, reacting.	Rotates hand, without touching the blade and lunges with a cut to flank.

(Left-handed/right-handed combination: Fencer B lunges with a cut to chest.)

3	In the on-guard position. Gives agreed signal for the training sequence to begin.	In the on-guard position. Takes a small step forward, then a small step backward.
	Steps forward, following. • The fencers are now at lunge distance for a cut to head.	Does a beat attack and lunges immediately with a cut to head, attacking into the preparation.

Simple and Compound Counter-Attacks

A stop-cut is a premeditated action of second intention. It is not done as a reaction.

Build technique by learning to cut lightly behind the guard at close quarters. Tap the guard first near the blade, continue tapping and gradually moving the hand laterally until the cuts are landing cleanly on the wrist with angulation, then move back to the starting point. Try this several times. A stop-cut is usually followed by a step backward. This is done by moving the rear foot (reaching back with the toe and maintaining the body and head upright) as the cut lands, then moving back the front foot to complete the step backward. In the event of the cut being unsuccessful, a parry and riposte can also be introduced.

Let us consider some real situations where a stop-cut might be used, for example a badly executed compound attack. Start at step and lunge distance for a cut to head.

Fencer A	**Fencer B**
1 In the on-guard position. Steps forward, does a head–flank compound attack, takes the hand back a little after feinting to head, then proceeds to flank.	In the on-guard position. Attempts successive parries of quinte and tierce. • Fencer B observes the exposure of the wrist during the attack.

(Left-handed/right-handed combination: Fencer A does a head–chest compound attack. Fencer B attempts successive parries of quinte and quarte.

Fencer A	**Fencer B**
2 In the on-guard position Steps forward, does a head–flank compound attack, takes the hand back a little after feinting to head, then proceeds to flank.	In the on-guard position Executes a stop-cut to wrist on the withdrawal of the hand, then steps backward. • The step has created a period of fencing time.

(Left-handed/right-handed combination: Fencer A does head–chest compound attack.)

As the attacker advances, try the stop-cut with a disengagement. A stop-cut with cutover sometimes hits the guard. Also the disengagement action tends to give a clear signal to the referee. Start at step and lunge distance for a cut to chest.

Fencer A	**Fencer B**
1 In the on-guard position. Steps forward, extending the sword arm with the landing of the rear foot and lunges with a cut to chest.	In the on-guard position. No response.

Next:

Fencer A	**Fencer B**
2 In the on-guard position. Steps forward, extending the sword arm.	In the on-guard position. Does an angulated stop-cut to the wrist on the advance and steps backward as the attack commences.
Lunges as before.	• Fencer B has gained a period of fencing time.
3 In the on-guard position. Steps forward, extending the sword arm.	In the on-guard position. Does an angulated stop-cut to the wrist on the advance. Parries quarte and ripostes with a cut to head (instead of stepping backward).

> • Fencer B has gained a period of fencing time.

To successfully perform a compound stop-cut requires an element of surprise. Start with a simple counter-attack at lunge distance for a cut to flank.

Fencer A	**Fencer B**
1 In the on-guard position. Presents hand in pronation, beginning a cut to flank.	In the on-guard position. Practises a stop-cut to the top of the wrist, moving the rear foot backward with the cut to the wrist. • The body position stays the same. The front foot moves backward to complete the step after the stop-cut lands. • Fencer B has created a period of fencing time.

Once this is mastered, Fencer A adds a parry and riposte.

2 In the on-guard position. Presents hand in pronation, beginning a cut to flank. Parries tierce. Ripostes with a lunge and cut to head.	In the on-guard position. Attempts a stop-cut to the top of the wrist.

When ready, Fencer B does a compound counter-attack.

3 In the on-guard position. Presents hand in pronation, beginning a cut to flank. Parries tierce, anticipating.	In the on-guard position. Does a very short feint to the top of the wrist. Does a disengagement around the guard to cut lightly to the top of the wrist, then steps backward to create a period of fencing time.

(Left-handed/right-handed combination: in 1.,2. and 3., Fencer A presents the hand in pronation beginning a cut to chest.)

Methods of Dealing with Counter-Attacks

These are:

- parry it
- pull your hand back, so that the attack misses
- put the counter-attack out of time.

A small (forward) parry of quarte will prevent a cut to wrist. This is sometimes called a half-parry. My own master, Prof. H T Bracewell, was taught this under the term 'offensive–defensive parry'. This is done by simply turning the guard toward the blade. If the stop-cut still lands, this means you are too close. As the defender's hand moves forward, the area of the defensive box being defended reduces. Parries taken in this way are taken sooner. The riposte covers a shorter distance, since the blade is closer to the target. This can also be used against a compound attack. The half-parry can be used in response to the feints, because to commit to a full parry at an early stage would make it difficult to parry the final action successfully.

Start with a parry and riposte, at step and lunge distance for a cut to head.

Fencer A	Fencer B
1 In the on-guard position. Moves hand to tierce.	In the on-guard position. Steps forward and feints a cut to chest.
Attempts a stop-cut to wrist.	• The fencers are now at lunge distance for a cut to head.
	Turns the guard toward quarte parry and ripostes with a lunge and cut to head.

(Left-handed/right-handed combination: Fencer B turns the guard toward tierce.)

Pull the hand back.

Fencer A	Fencer B
2 In the on-guard position. Moves hand to tierce.	In the on-guard position. Steps forward and feints a cut to chest.
Attempts a stop-cut to wrist.	Pulls the hand back and continues with a lunge and cut to head. • The stop-cut misses.
Put the counter-attack out of time.	
3 In the on-guard position. Moves hand to tierce.	In the on-guard position. Begins a feint cut to chest; the front foot moves forward only. The heel lands.
Attempts a stop-cut to wrist.	The front foot only continues forward; the rear foot has not moved. Fencer B lunges with a cut to the forearm. • Fencer A's hit lands out of time.

Actions Using the Point and the Use of the Line

Use of the line: we can stop-point, stop-cut, beat and parry from this position. The arm and blade (together) must be straight, threatening only the high line. If you take the point from the target during dérobement (which is the successful evasion of an intended attack au fer, or prise de fer), you loose priority. If you convert the point action to a cut, you loose priority.

Start with skills training, practising counter-disengagements (little circles) around the blade and guard. The emphasis here is on increasingly smaller movements.

Start at lunge distance for a cut to head.

Fencer A	Fencer B
1	Begins with the sword arm extended.
Gives agreed signal for the training sequence to begin.	Steps backward with arm still extended.

The use of the line.

<table>
<tr><td></td><td>• The fencers are now at step and lunge distance for a cut to head.</td></tr>
</table>

Steps forward, attempts to gather the blade with counter-tierce, or seconde.
• The fencers are now at lunge distance for a cut to head.

Does a neat small dérobement.

Finishes the attack, lunging with a cut to head.
• Both hits land.

• Fencer B's hit has priority.

Next as before, but Fencer A does a jump instead of a step, obliging Fencer B to do the dérobement much faster.

Practise a compound dérobement, starting at lunge distance for a cut to head.

Fencer A	**Fencer B**
2	Begins with the sword arm extended.
Gives agreed signal for the training sequence to begin.	Steps backward with arm still extended. • The fencers are now at step

	and lunge distance for a cut to head.
Steps forward, attempts to gather the blade with counter-tierce. • The fencers are now at lunge distance for a cut to head.	Does a neat small dérobement and steps backward.
Steps forward and attempts to take the blade with seconde. • The fencers are once again at lunge distance for a cut to head.	Does a neat small dérobement.
Finishes the attack, lunging with a cut to head. • Both hits land.	• Fencer B's hit has priority.

The blade is already in a good position to do a surprise stop-cut.

Fencer A	**Fencer B**
3	Begins with the sword arm extended.
In the on-guard position. Steps forward.	Stop-cuts to wrist and steps backward immediately.

Stop-cutting from seconde is a similar idea.

There are several ways of dealing with the point in line:

• beat the blade
• engage the blade (or engage the blade and beat)
• ignore it, just cutting to the wrist.

Circular beats are useful in momentarily exposing the extended target. The circular blade action should be performed continuously, with no pause between the beat and cut to wrist. Start at a distance where a cut can be performed on the wrist.

Fencer A	Fencer B
1 Begins with the sword arm extended.	Does a circular beat on the top of the blade and cuts above the wrist
2 Begins with the sword arm extended.	Does a circular beat on the underside of the blade and cuts below the wrist.

Exploiting the Simultaneous Attack Situation

Start at a distance equivalent to that between the on-guard lines on the piste (the field of play), which is 4m. The simultaneous actions will be initiated by a verbal or visual signal. A bout is started by the referee saying the word 'play'.

Fencer A	Fencer B
1 In the on-guard position. Gives agreed signal for simultaneous attacks to begin, then steps forward and lunges with a cut to head. • Both hits land. • Neither fencer has priority.	In the on-guard position. Steps forward and lunges with a cut to head.
2 In the on-guard position. Gives agreed signal for simultaneous attacks to begin, steps forward and lunges with a cut to head.	In the on-guard position. Takes a short step forward, stop-cuts to wrist and steps backward.
3 In the on-guard position. Gives agreed signal for simultaneous attacks to begin, steps forward and lunges with a cut to head.	In the on-guard position. Steps forward, begins to lunge, does a high beat parry of quarte during the course of the lunge, finishes with a cut to head.

Renewed Offence

If the attack is renewed into the original line, this is called a remise. If it is renewed into a different line, this is called a redoublement. It is also possible to remise a stop-cut.

Start at lunge distance for a cut to head. First:

Fencer A	**Fencer B**
1 In the on-guard position. Lowers the blade by rotating the hand a little in pronation, offering an opening line.	Lunges with a cut to head.
Parries quinte.	Recovers backward to guard. • The fencers are once again at lunge distance for a cut to head.
Lunges with the riposte with a cut to head.	

Then:

Fencer A	**Fencer B**
2 In the on-guard position. Lowers the blade by rotating the hand a little in pronation.	Lunges with a cut to head.
Takes a small step backward. Parries quinte, pauses briefly (which is what happens when stepping backward with a parry). Takes a small step forward.	Does a remise cut to head as the opponent steps forward. Recovers backward to guard. • The fencers are once again at lunge distance for a cut to head.
Lunges with a cut to head.	• Fencer B is awarded the hit.

If the cut is made to the wrist, then this would be called a redoublement. Start at lunge distance for a cut to head.

Fencer A	**Fencer B**
1 In the on-guard position. Lowers the blade by rotating the hand a little in pronation.	Lunges with a cut to head.

Parries quinte, pauses briefly.	Immediately does a redoublement to wrist, still on lunge.

2 In the on-guard position. Lowers the blade by rotating the hand a little in pronation.

Lunges with a cut to head.

Parries quinte, pauses briefly.	Immediately does a redoublement to wrist, still on lunge. Recovers backward to guard. • The fencers are once again at lunge distance for a cut to head.
Ripostes to head with a lunge.	Parries quinte and ripostes with a cut to head.

Next, a reprise. Start at lunge distance for a cut to head.

Fencer A	**Fencer B**
1 In the on-guard position. Lowers the blade by rotating the hand a little in pronation.	Lunges with a cut to head.
Steps backward to avoid being hit.	Lifts up rear foot to return (forward) to guard. The fencers are now at lunge distance for a cut to head. Lunges with a cut to head. • Fencer B's actions must be continuous.

A compound reverse reprise:

2 In the on-guard position. Lowers the blade by rotating the hand a little in pronation.	In the on-guard position. Lunges with a deliberately short cut to head.
Parries quinte, then lowers the blade.	Remises to head, extending the lunge a little. Returns to guard with arm straight, front foot lightly touching the ground.

- The fencers are once again at lunge distance for a cut to head. Begins to lunge with a feint cut to head.

Parries quinte, responding.

Rotates the hand during the course of the lunge with a cut to flank.

(Left-handed/right-handed combination: Fencer B lunges head–chest.)

Continuity Hitting

You will need a sleeve and plastron for this exercise. Fencer A should try to keep the point up and maintain the on-guard position correctly, as gradually dropping the point will lead to unnecessarily large actions. Start slowly, with one or two actions, adding the others progressively until you can do them all one after the other without stopping. Gradually speed up, but concentrate on accuracy.

Fencer B's first action is a beat on the forte (lower third of the blade). Parries are normally performed here and beats done on the top two-thirds. This is the way it was taught to me, and as a training routine it seems to work quite spontaneously. If you feel that to beat in this way, even for training purposes, is not appropriate, Fencer B can begin simply with the cut to wrist (no beat). The reader is free to decide.

Start at a distance where you can just cut to head. Let it flow.

Fencer A	**Fencer B**
1 In the on-guard position. Gives agreed signal for the training sequence to begin.	In the on-guard position. A cutting edge beat to forte of blade, cuts to top of wrist.
	Back-edge beat in the centre of the blade, cuts to top shoulder.
	Back-edge beat and cuts to outside cheek.
	Circular beat in the centre of the blade and cuts to head.
	Circular beat in the centre of

the blade and cuts to inside cheek.

Circular beat in the centre of the blade and does through cut to chest.
• Be careful to finish cleanly through the flank.

Lifts the end of the back-edge of the blade to cut lightly under the wrist.

Rotates under the guard to beat in the centre of the front edge of the blade and cuts to head.

Returns to guard.

Places the point of sabre on opponent's chest by extending the sword arm.

(Left-handed/right-handed combination: Fencer A holds the sabre in the opposite hand, then proceeds as above.)

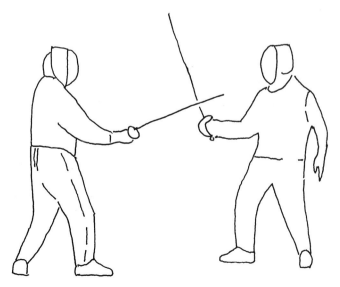

Cutting edge beat to forte of blade.

Cuts to top of wrist.

Back-edge beat.

Cuts to shoulder/top of arm.

Back-edge beat.

Cuts to outside cheek.

Cuts to head.

Cuts to inside cheek.

Through cut to chest.

Cut under wrist.

Rotates under the guard to beat the front edge of the blade.

Cuts to head.

Returns to guard.

Places point on opponent's chest.

Broken Time

To be effective, broken time must be a surprise action. The defender effectively tells himself or herself not to move. Start with a few compound attacks, causing a reaction of successive parries.

At lunge distance for a cut to head:

Fencer A	**Fencer B**
1 In the on-guard position. Lowers the blade by rotating the hand a little in pronation. Parries quinte and ripostes to head.	In the on-guard position. Lunges with a cut to head.

Now we have a reason for Fencer B to do a compound attack.

Fencer A	**Fencer B**
2 In the on-guard position. Lowers the blade by rotating the hand a little in pronation.	In the on-guard position. Lunges with a feint to head.
Parries quinte.	Rotates the hand during the course of the lunge and lunges with a cut to flank.

(Left-handed/right-handed combination: Fencer B finishes with a cut to chest.)

3 In the on-guard position. Lowers the blade by rotating the hand a little in pronation.	In the on-guard position. Lunges with a feint to head.
Parries quinte early.	Rotates the hand during the course of the lunge and lunges with a cut to flank.
Parries tierce and ripostes with a cut to head. • This is a late parry.	

(Left-handed/right-handed combination: Fencer B finishes with a cut to chest. Fencer A parries quarte and ripostes with a cut to head.)

Now a surprise broken-time attack:

4 In the on-guard position. Lowers the blade by rotating the hand a little in pronation.	In the on-guard position. Lunges with a feint to head.
Parries quinte, then tierce, anticipating.	Pulls hand back to tierce as the lunge finishes; the leading foot lands.
Fencer A freezes momentarily in tierce.	Continues with a cut to head.

(Left-handed/right-handed combination: Fencer A parries quinte then quarte, anticipating.)

Angulated Actions

Much in sabre is angulated. You can angulate around a guard, or around a parry. Angulation is also particularly helpful when fencing at close quarters. Angulation shortens reach and can be used on:
• attacks
• ripostes
• counter-attacks.

The cut to wrist around the guard means that the guard may not be touched at all, because, technically speaking, this would create a cut that is a remise.
    Start at step and lunge distance for a cut to head.

Fencer A	Fencer B
In the on-guard position. Lowers the blade by rotating the hand a little in pronation.	In the on-guard position. Steps forward with a feint to head.
Steps backward. • The fencers are once again at step and lunge distance for a cut to head, or lunge distance for a cut to the extended target.	Lunges and reverts to an angulated cut to wrist.

At lunge distance for a cut to head:

	Fencer A	Fencer B
1	In the on-guard position. Lunges with a cut to head.	In the on-guard position. Parries quinte and ripostes to flank.
2	In the on-guard position. Lunges with a cut to head.	In the on-guard position. Parries quinte and ripostes to flank.
	Parries tierce on the lunge and ripostes with a cut to head.	

(Left-handed/right-handed combination: for 1. and 2., Fencer B ripostes to chest.)

3   In the on-guard position.   In the on-guard position.
Lunges with a cut to head.   Parries quinte and starts to
riposte.

Parries tierce on the lunge.   Finishes with an angulate cut
under the parry to the wrist.

(Left-handed/right-handed combination: Fencer B ripostes to chest.
Fencer A parries quarte.)

Attacking into a preparation.

CHAPTER SIX

Coaching Sabre

A Few Thoughts

The standard of the student will to some extent reflect the abilities of the coach. The student will learn from the coach's knowledge, sense of rhythm, reflexes and blade presentations. The teaching position is similar to foil, but the coach works predominantly with absence of blade.

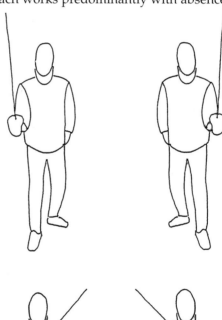

The teaching position.

Lowers blade, inviting cut to head.

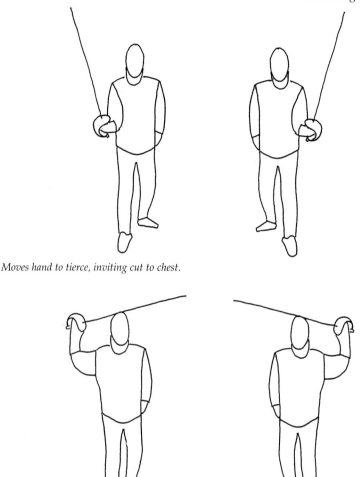

Moves hand to tierce, inviting cut to chest.

Lifts hand to quinte, inviting cut to flank.

More time tends to be spent teaching the hit than is the case at foil, because the various target areas each require a different hand position. Cuts are studied separately and at various distances: straight arm; short lunge; longer lunge; short step and lunge; two steps and lunge; balestra lunge; step balestra lunge; and many other footwork combinations. When teaching defence at sabre, the angle of the coach's guard, when presenting a feint or cut, gives an early indication of the line to be defended. This is a kind of language between the coach and the student. If the guard is presented vertically, the feint or cut is being presented to the head. If the guard is horizontal, with the knuckles turned up, then the feint or cut is being presented to flank, and so on.

Situations in fencing evolve through action and response. Learn each of these routines, then Fencer A (the coach) can vary the responses.

Start at step and lunge distance for a cut to head.

Sabre fencing is demonstrated to a group and the coach explains the actions.

Fencer A	**Fencer B**
1 Begins with the arm extended.	In the on-guard position. Steps forward and lightly engages the blade in quarte and lunges with a cut to head.
2 Begins with the arm extended.	In the on-guard position. Steps forward and attempts the engagement.
Lowers the blade to avoid the engagement. • The fencers are now at lunge distance for a cut to cheek.	Beats the blade in seconde and lunges with a cut to outside cheek.

(Left-handed/right-handed combination: Fencer B lunges with a cut to inside cheek.)

3 Begins with the arm extended.	In the on-guard position. Steps forward and attempts the engagement.
Does a cutover with a lunge to head, attacking suddenly into the preparation.	Parries quinte and ripostes with a cut to head (second intention).

The following exercises are useful in developing a better technical understanding of the use of preparations.

A single blade preparation at step and lunge distance for a cut to head:

Fencer A	**Fencer B**
1 Presents the blade a little forward of tierce.	In the on-guard position. Steps forward and lightly engages the blade in quarte and lunges with a cut to head.

A double blade preparation:

Fencer A	**Fencer B**
2 Presents the blade a little forward of tierce.	In the on-guard position. Steps forward and engages the blade in quarte, rotates the blade (through counter-tierce, a change of engagement) and moves the hand laterally toward tierce.
Parries quinte, anticipating.	Lunges with a cut to flank.
3 Presents the blade a little forward of tierce.	In the on-guard position. Steps forward and engages the blade in quarte. Suddenly applies greater pressure on the same side of the blade and lunges with a cut to outside cheek.

(Left-handed/right-handed combination: Fencer B lunges with a cut to inside cheek.)

Counter-riposte training is good for developing control of the hand. Do this sequence slowly, gradually gaining speed. The parries should be performed with the blades only lightly making contact, the riposte following spontaneously without a pause, starting at lunge distance for a cut to flank.

Fencer A	**Fencer B**
In the on-guard position. Steps forward and cuts to flank.	In the on-guard position. Parries tierce and ripostes to flank.
Parries tierce and ripostes with a cut to head.	Parries quinte and ripostes with a cut to head.
Parries quinte and ripostes with a cut to chest.	Parries quarte and ripostes with a cut to head.

(Left-handed/right-handed combination: Fencer A steps forward and cuts to chest. Fencer B parries quarte and ripostes to flank ... Fencer A parries quinte and ripostes to flank. Lastly, Fencer B parries tierce and ripostes with a cut to head.)

PART THREE
Épée

CHAPTER SEVEN

Épée Training

Introduction

The épée is the modern version of the historical duelling sword. The valid target at this weapon is the whole body. The épée is heavier than the foil and has a rigid bi-angular blade, with a larger guard to protect the hand from a valid hit. Hits are scored with the point only. Fencers do not need to wear metallic jackets. Hits are registered by electronic scoring apparatus. A coloured light is registered when a hit lands. If you hit the floor, a coloured light comes on, unless you are fencing on a copper piste. A double hit occurs when both fencers' hits land simultaneously. The fencing phrasing is not critical in épée since the first person to hit scores a point. Hits are separated by 1/25 of a second. The character of the weapon is affected by the extensive target. The possibility of double hits poses a problem in defence and also offers opportunities for counter-offensive actions. The épéeist must be able to hit without being hit. Adapted foil actions make up the technical basis of épée. As with foil, the hit must arrive with the character of penetration. If the point slides past the target without registering a hit this is called passé.

The épée target.

Although usually competing in their own separate competitions, men and women can fence épée together on equal terms. Veteran fencers can fence into old age, as in the case of Colonel Hay, pictured below.

Men and women fence together on equal terms.

Bert Bracewell (left) and Colonel Hay (right). This photograph was taken on Colonel Hay's birthday after taking a half-an-hour's fencing lesson at Meadowbank Sports Centre, Edinburgh. Bert always said that when he gave Colonel Hay a fencing lesson he learned as much back in return.

On Guard and Footwork

The on-guard position in épée is similar to foil, but the fencer may close this stance a little if the leading leg is felt to be vulnerable. The hand is held further forward, with the forearm horizontal behind the large bell guard for protection. The point is angled in a little, inward and downward. If you find your elbow sticking out, supinate your hand a little more and the elbow will tuck in. Épée is fenced toe to toe generally, but some fencers move over a little in order to look for angulated hits to hand/forearm.

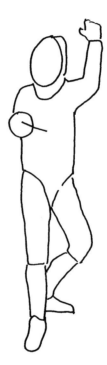

The on-guard position.

Fencing measure at épée is where the opponent can hit the extended target (hand) with a lunge. The lunge, recovery stepping forward and backward are as for foil. The lunge tends to be not as long. It is typically fenced with absence of blade, which allows both fencers to close their outside line of sixte to protect the outer arm.

There is a stronger spring in the tip of an electric épée, compared to that of an electric foil. The character of hit is more like that which would occur during a real dual. One-hit épée (where the first to score one hit wins) is perhaps the purest form. Unlike the other two weapons, it is acceptable to attack your opponent's toe. Hits on the mask are valid, but can be painful to receive. Fence as you would be fenced unto.

Control of the Weapon

The grip is similar to that at foil. Like foil, French-design or orthopaedic handles can be used. Some fencers like to hold the end of a French handle, to extend their reach, which is allowed. The end of the French handle is called the 'pommel', and the action of holding the French handle in this way is referred to as pommelling. The pommel is placed in the centre of the palm with the thumb and the forefinger gripping the top and underside of the handle. The other three forefingers are wrapped around the pommel.

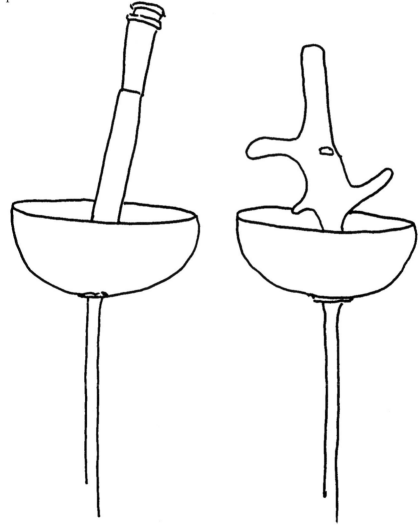

A French handle (left) and an orthopaedic handle (right).

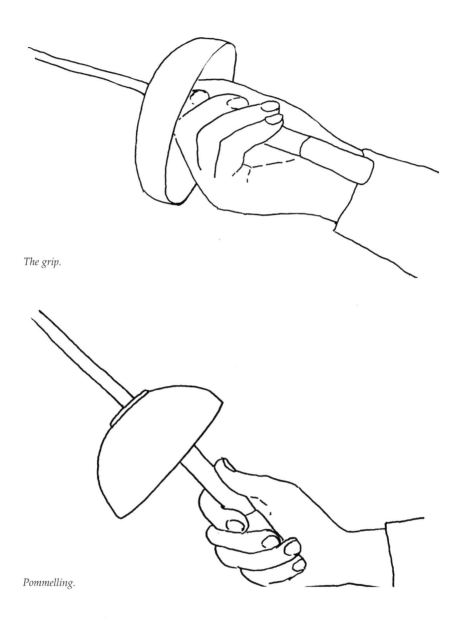

The grip.

Pommelling.

When attacking, the arm should be fully extended and relaxed, with the hand slightly in supination and slightly higher than the shoulder, before the front foot moves. The hand must not drop at the end of the lunge and should remain high enough to get protection from the guard. After the hit, relax the hand and raise it slightly to free the tension in the blade. The blade has a slight downward curve. On recovery to on guard, the arm remains straight and relaxed, with the point in line with the target.

The lunge.

Always use a protective sleeve when practising hits to the arm. Start at a distance where you can just hit the hand/forearm with a straight arm. Offer an easy target to begin with, then gradually close it up.

Fencer A	Fencer B
In the on-guard position.	In the on-guard position.
Slowly turns the hand a little toward quarte, exposing the hand/forearm.	Straightens the sword arm and hits neatly with the point to hand/forearm, just bending the blade of the épée.

Hits neatly with point to wrist.

Practising a hit with point to arm.

Now work through a training routine with three hits in succession. Start at épée fencing measure. Fencing measure at épée is where the opponent can hit the extended target (hand/forearm) with a lunge.

Fencer A	**Fencer B**
In the on-guard position. Slowly turns the hand a little toward sixte, exposing the hand/forearm.	In the on-guard position. Does a short lunge with a hit to hand/forearm. Moves the foot a little further forward and hits further up the arm. Moves the foot a little further forward (to a full lunge) and hits the upper arm.

Simple Attacks

The simple attack, direct or indirect, is correctly executed when the straightening of the arm proceeds the initiation of the lunge or the flèche. The épée target, which cannot be completely covered, ensures that the épéeist is a cautious attacker. The types of simple attacks are as for foil. However, the use of the cutover at épée is restricted, since this temporarily leaves the under arm exposed, although it can be used as a surprise attack.

Start at épée fencing measure.

	Fencer A	**Fencer B**
1	In the on-guard position. Steps forward and turns the hand a little toward quarte. • The fencers are now at straight arm distance for a hit to hand/forearm.	In the on-guard position. Straightens the sword arm and hits with the point to hand/forearm.
	Lightly taps the blade as a signal and steps backward.	Returns to guard.
2	In the on-guard position. Turns the hand a little toward quarte (no step forward).	In the on-guard position. Straightens the sword arm and lunges with a hit to hand/forearm.

- The fencers are still at lunge distance for a hit to hand/forearm.

Lightly taps the blade as a signal.	Recovers to guard.

The return to guard technique is similar to that of foil.

3 In the on-guard position. Steps backward and turns the hand a little toward quarte.	In the on-guard position. Straightens the sword arm and steps forward and lunges with a hit to the hand/forearm.

Now try a disengagement at épée fencing measure.

Fencer A	**Fencer B**
1 In the on-guard position. Steps forward and moves the blade slightly toward sixte. • The fencers are now at straight arm distance for a hit to hand/forearm.	In the on-guard position. Disengages under the blade, then straightens the arm and hits to hand/forearm.
2 In the on-guard position. Moves the blade lightly toward sixte. • The fencers are still at lunge distance for a hit to hand/forearm.	In the on-guard position. Disengages under the blade, straightens the arm and lunges with a hit to hand/forearm as the front foot lands. • An alternative finish might be an attack to the knee.
3 In the on-guard position. Steps backward and the moves blade lightly toward sixte.	In the on-guard position. Straightens the sword arm with a disengagement and steps forward (together), then lunges with a hit to hand/forearm.

Attacking with a disengagement.

Parries and Ripostes

The parry is a defensive action made with the blade to prevent the attack from landing. The principle of defence is the opposition of forte to foible. The riposte is the offensive action made by the fencer who has successfully parried the attack. This can be direct, indirect or compound.

Parries and ripostes are often to the target that is lying closest to the point. With the bent arm (foil-like), parries and ripostes are used against a surprise attack which results in close quarters, or when using a ceding or opposition parry (which are both defences against prise de fer). Attacks to the hand/forearm are parried with small movements of the guard, up and down and from side to side. This is sometimes referred to as the 'cone of defence'. The types of parries are as for foil, but with épée all parries should be taken with the hand well forward (half extension). In this position, it is easier to cover the extended target.

Épéeists generally favour the lines of sixte and octave. Where quarte is used, the riposte will almost invariably be with opposition, holding on to the blade. Parries can occasionally take the form of beat parries. If done at close quarters, then the only effective response is to the body.

From quarte, the riposte will almost invariably be with opposition.

A circular parry (counter-parry) of sixte, performed at a distance where the tip of the blade can be laid on the guard.

Fencer A	**Fencer B**
In the on-guard position.	In the on-guard position.
Lays the tip of the blade on the (top) inside of the guard.	Practises the circular action with the fingers, with a little extra supination at the end to get on top of the opponent's blade.

A semicircular parry of octave:

Fencer A	Fencer B
In the on-guard position.	In the on-guard position.
Lays the tip of the blade on the (lower) inside of the guard.	Practises a semicircular parry of octave.

In octave, the point is already well positioned for a hit to leg.

Now Fencer A places the point on top (and just past) the guard, Fencer B practises lifting the guard upward to protect the hand/forearm. Fencer A holds Fencer B's point to ensure that it stays exactly where it was. Fencer A (still holding Fencer B's point) places the point above, below, outside and inside the guard (randomly). Fencer B practises moving the guard (in correct response) to protect the hand/forearm.

Fencer A releases the point, continuing now at lunge distance for a hit to hand/forearm.

Fencer B uses the coquille to protect the hand/forearm (a coquille is the name for the bell-shaped guard on a foil or épée).

	Fencer A	Fencer B
1	In the on-guard position. Lunges to top of the hand/fore-arm.	In the on-guard position. Lifts the guard upward to pro-tect the extended target, ripostes to the nearest available target.
2	In the on-guard position. Lunges to inside of hand/fore-arm.	In the on-guard position. Moves the guard laterally to protect the extended target, ripostes to the nearest available target.
3	In the on-guard position. Lunges to outside of hand/forearm.	In the on-guard position. Moves the guard laterally to protect the extended target, ripostes to the nearest available target.
4	In the on-guard position. Lunges underneath the hand/forearm.	In the on-guard position. Lowers the guard downward to protect the extended target, ripostes to the nearest available target.

Compound Attacks

A compound attack comprises one or more feints. Compound attacks are similar to that used in foil. These are done at a greater distance, with absence of blade. We shall start with some skills training, in order to develop finger control.

Start at a distance where Fencer B can touch the opponent's hand/forearm with a straight arm.

Fencer A	Fencer B
In the on-guard position.	In the on-guard position. Straightens the sword arm. Lays tip of blade on the wrist (inside).
Moves guard a little toward quarte.	Does a small disengagement and places the tip of the blade back on the wrist.
Moves the guard a little toward sixte.	Does a small disengagement and places the tip of the blade back on the wrist.
And so on.	

Allow the point to trail just around the guard, keeping the actions as small as possible. Now add (small) circular actions of counter-sixte and then attempt to take the blade with octave. Fencer B must now respond to different (unannounced) blade actions.

Now try a compound attack at full épée fencing measure.

	Fencer A	Fencer B
1	In the on-guard position. Moves the blade lightly toward sixte.	In the on-guard position. Disengages and lunges with the point to the hand/forearm.
2	In the on-guard position. Moves the blade lightly toward sixte.	In the on-guard position. Disengages and starts to lunge.
	Parries counter-sixte.	Counter-disengages progressively during the course of the

		lunge and hits to hand/forearm.
3	In the on-guard position. Moves the blade lightly toward sixte and takes a small step backward.	In the on-guard position. Takes a small step forward with the disengagement and starts to lunge.
	Parries counter-sixte.	Counter-disengages progressively during the course of the lunge and hits to hand/forearm.
4	In the on-guard position. Moves the blade lightly toward sixte and takes a small step backward.	In the on-guard position. Takes a small step forward with the disengagement and starts to lunge.
	Parries counter-sixte.	Counter-disengages progressively during the course of the lunge and feints to hand/forearm.
	Parries quarte, late.	Hits to leg.

An alternative to this for Fencer B might be to hit to toe.

Now try parrying octave at épée fencing measure.

Fencer A	**Fencer B**
In the on-guard position. Moves the blade lightly toward sixte.	In the on-guard position. Disengages and feints to the five o'clock position next to the guard.
Parries octave.	The point trails around the guard, without touching, and Fencer B lunges to top of hand/forearm.

(Left-handed/right-handed combination: for a left hander the five o'clock position is inverted.)

In the same manner, attacks may be improvised to the underside of the hand/forearm, leg and foot. If Fencer A steps forward (closing distance) the final action of the compound attack may be launched to body.

Successive Parries and Ripostes

Successive parries are a response to a compound attack. For the hit to leg, simply lift the point using the fingers and place it on. Start at épée fencing measure.

Fencer A	Fencer B
1 In the on-guard position. Gives agreed signal for the training sequence to begin.	In the on-guard position. Moves the blade lightly toward sixte.
Disengages and lunges to hand/forearm.	Parries counter-sixte.
Counter-disengages progressively during the course of the lunge and lunges to leg.	Parries octave and ripostes with point to leg.
2 In the on-guard position. Gives agreed signal for the training sequence to begin.	In the on-guard position. Moves the blade lightly toward sixte.
Disengages and lunges with the point at the five o'clock position of the guard.	Attempts to parry octave.
Trails the point around the guard progressively during the course of the lunge and lunges to top of hand/forearm.	Parries sixte and ripostes to upper arm, holding on to the blade.
3 In the on-guard position. Gives agreed signal for the training sequence to begin.	In the on-guard position. Moves the blade lightly toward sixte.
Disengages and lunges above the guard to hand/forearm.	Attempts to parry octave with a gathering action.

	Fencer A	Fencer B
	Trails the point around the guard progressively during the course of the lunge and lunges to top of hand/forearm.	Parries counter-octave and ripostes with point to leg, holding on to the blade.
4	In the on-guard position. Gives agreed signal for the training sequence to begin.	In the on-guard position. Moves the blade lightly toward sixte.
	Disengages and lunges above the guard to hand/forearm.	Attempts to parry octave with a gathering action.
	Trails the point around the guard progressively during the course of the lunge and lunges to top of hand/forearm.	Cuts the line diagonally to quarte with hand well forward and ripostes with opposition to arm.

Preparations

A preparation of attack is any movement that prepares the way. A list of typical preparations is included in Chapter 1 on foil training. The preparation is particularly useful at épée, because of the long fencing measure and the attacker's vulnerability to counter-attacks. Attacking the blade as a preparation will either deflect the opponent's point or get a reaction. This requires an element of surprise. The response to this preparation may well be a stop-hit rather than a parry, hence the importance of prises de fer, where in addition to deflecting the blade you can control it. Done correctly, the attacker should find no opposition from the opponent's blade.

Some blade preparations at full épée fencing measure, starting with the beat:

	Fencer A	**Fencer B**
1	In the on-guard position. Straightens the sword arm.	In the on-guard position. Beats the side of the blade, lunges and hits with the point to the forearm.
2	In the on-guard position. Straightens the sword arm.	In the on-guard position. Beats the top of the blade, lunges and hits with the point to the top of the forearm.

	Fencer A	Fencer B
3	In the on-guard position. Gives the agreed signal for the training sequence to begin. Straightens the sword arm, responding to the opponent's cutover.	In the on-guard position. Does cutover, immediately followed by a beat to the top of the blade. Lunges with a hit to forearm.
4	In the on-guard position. Steps forward. • The fencers are now at lunge distance for a hit to body.	In the on-guard position. Immediately does a beat and lunges to body.

An envelopment at épée fencing measure.

	Fencer A	**Fencer B**
1	In the on-guard position. Straightens the sword arm.	In the on-guard position. Gathers the blade with counter-sixte, immediately gathers a second time with the same circular action, straightens the sword arm and lunges with a hit to upper arm. • Ensure domination of the top of the blade.
2	In the on-guard position. Straightens the sword arm.	In the on-guard position. Gathers the blade in octave, immediately gathers a second time with a circular action and lunges with a hit to upper arm. • Ensure domination of the underside of the blade.

A bind at épée fencing measure:

	Fencer A	**Fencer B**
1	In the on-guard position. Straightens the sword arm.	In the on-guard position. Gathers the blade with counter-sixte, then binds diagonally to septime and lunges with a hit to leg.

Counter-Attacks

A counter-attack is an offensive action delivered on the opponent's attack in such a way that it arrests it. It can be used against a badly executed attack, or against a fencer who misjudges distance. Some épéeists stop-hit in order to obtain a double hit, when the score is in

The forearm is vulnerable to a stop-hit.

their favour. A time-hit (which is a stop-hit with opposition) is a premeditated action, delivered into the last action of the attack that is proceeding into a known line. The attacker is effectively impaled on the point.

Start by practising hits to hand/forearm. If you find it difficult, you can start by hitting nearer the inner crease at the meeting of the forearm and upper arm, then gradually work back. Stand close enough to deliver a hit to hand/forearm by just straightening the sword arm.

Fencer A	Fencer B
In the on-guard position. Either offers an opening or attempts to take the blade.	In the on-guard position. Practises applying hits to hand/forearm/arm by straightening into the opening or evading the blade.

Try a stop-hit at full épée fencing measure, almost toe to toe, the foot moved over slightly to improve the angle of the stop-hit to hand/forearm.

	Fencer A	Fencer B
1	In the on-guard position. Steps forward.	In the on-guard position. Steps backward, responding quickly. • The fencers are once again at lunge distance for a hit to hand/forearm.
	Lunges with the point to the hand/forearm.	
2	In the on-guard position. Steps forward as before.	In the on-guard position. Stop-hits to hand/forearm, then steps backward.

A time-hit at épée fencing measure:

Fencer A	Fencer B
In the on-guard position. Steps forward and lunges with the point to the hand/forearm.	In the on-guard position. Does a counter-sixte gathering action on the opponent's blade, straightening the arm at the same time, with a hit on the forearm. • This done as one continuous action.

Counter-Time

Counter-time is an action made by an attacker on the opponent's attempt to stop-hit. To draw the stop-hit, start at full épée fencing measure, almost toe to toe, the foot moved over slightly to improve the angle of the stop-hit to hand/forearm.

	Fencer A	Fencer B
1	In the on-guard position. Gives agreed signal for the training sequence to begin.	In the on-guard position. Takes a small step forward. A small step ensures that there is time to form the parry.
	Attempts a stop-hit to forearm.	Practises a parry of counter-sixte.
2	In the on-guard position. Gives agreed signal for the training sequence to begin.	In the on-guard position. Takes a small step forward.
	Attempts a stop-hit to forearm. Steps backward. • The fencers are once again at lunge distance for a hit to hand/forearm.	Parries counter-sixte. Lunges with riposte to hand/forearm.
3	In the on-guard position. Gives agreed signal for the training sequence to begin.	In the on-guard position. Takes a small step forward.

Attempts a stop-hit to forearm.	Parries counter-sixte.
Steps backward. • The fencers are now at lunge distance for a hit to hand/forearm, or a flèche to the body.	Flèches with the riposte to body.

Renewed Offence

A renewed offence is principally remise if it remains in the original line, or redoublement if it ends up in a different line. Alternatively, it can be a reprise, which is a renewal of attack that passes through the on-guard position.

Start at épée fencing measure, almost toe to toe, the foot moved over slightly for the hit to hand/forearm.

The remise:

Fencer A	Fencer B
In the on-guard position. Gives agreed signal for the training sequence to begin.	In the on-guard position. Lunges and attempts to hit the hand/forearm.
Parries counter-sixte.	Stays on the lunge.
Releases the blade, attempting a response.	Does remise to the hand/fore-arm. • No need to move the point.

The reprise:

Fencer A	Fencer B
In the on-guard position. Gives agreed signal for the training sequence to begin.	In the on-guard position. Starts to lunge.
Steps backward to avoid being hit.	Finishes the lunge, brings up rear foot (three-quarters of the way), and does a short lunge with a hit to hand/forearm.

The redoublement:

Fencer A	**Fencer B**
In the on-guard position. Gives agreed signal for the training sequence to begin.	In the on-guard position. Does a short lunge.
Parries counter-sixte and pauses.	Immediately disengages to the hand/forearm, extending to the full lunge.

CHAPTER EIGHT

Advanced Épée Training

Introduction

Much that is good in épée is characterized by thrusts to the forearm, counter-offensive actions and remises. Similarities between foil and épée include that they are both thrusting weapons and both use the same system of positions and movements. Sabre and épée are similar in that they both include the arm, both require the assistance of the forearm and elbow to handle and control the weapon and both tend to come on guard at similar distances.

Speed can be subdivided into three categories – speed of foot, arm and point. The hand moves before the foot, otherwise the attacker is vulnerable to a counter-offensive hit on the bent arm during the advance. The foot moves, accelerating during a lunge, then the point bites forward, by turning the fingers with a downward action and the thumb pressing on top. Of the three, the speed of the point can be the most dramatic. The faster the point travels, the less contact area is required to depress it and score a hit. Hitting with the edge of the point can provide an effective, neat hit. Moving slower, the point needs to land head-on, with a greater area of contact.

Modified foil actions make up the technical basis of épée fencing, but they can be carried out against any part of the opponent's body target.

In this chapter, more emphasis is made on the use of combinations of fencing actions. Whilst we may start with a given topic, others may be introduced into the development of a series of actions to add a little depth.

Simple Attacks

Thrusts may be delivered directly (useful where a time advantage exists), with angulation, or with opposition. Simple thrusts with opposition (to body and arm) are often, but not exclusively, practised from the upper lines of engagement. Start by thrusting with opposition to chest, then to the shoulder/upper arm, as indicated in the exercise that follows.

At close quarters:

Fencer A	**Fencer B**
1 In the on-guard position. Slowly runs the blade down the outside of the opponent's blade.	In the on-guard position. Lifts the hand and places the point on arm, with opposition.
2 In the on-guard position. Slowly runs the blade down the inside of the opponent's blade.	In the on-guard position. Moves the hand toward quarte, lifts the hand and places the point on the arm, with opposition.

Move back a little so that Fencer B has to do a short lunge to arm.

Fencer A	**Fencer B**
3 In the on-guard position. Lightly makes contact with the outside of opponent's blade and straightens the sword arm.	In the on-guard position. Lifts the hand and places the point on the arm, as before but with a short lunge.
4 In the on-guard position. Lightly makes contact with the inside of opponent's blade and straightens the sword arm.	In the on-guard position. Moves the hand toward quarte, lifts the hand and places the point on the arm, as before but with a short lunge.

Training with the opponent's blade held in opposition ensures that the hand does not wander about. After a while, try doing a short lunge to hand/forearm with no blade contact, just lightly depressing the point. The hit should land neat and precise.

Fencer A	**Fencer B**
1 In the on-guard position. Slowly turns the hand a little toward quarte, exposing the outside hand/forearm.	In the on-guard position. Straightens the sword arm and does a short lunge to hand/forearm.

2 **Fencer A**	**Fencer B**
In the on-guard position. Slowly turns the hand a little	In the on-guard position. Straightens the sword arm and

toward quarte, exposing the outside hand/forearm.	places the point on the hand/forearm with a short lunge.
Turns the hand a little toward sixte, exposing inside hand/forearm.	Disengages and places the point on the hand/forearm, then returns to guard.
Turns the hand a little toward quarte, as before.	Disengages and lunges, placing the point on the hand/forearm, then returns to guard.
Turns the hand a little toward sixte, as before.	Disengages and lunges, placing point on the hand/forearm, returns to guard and steps backward.
Turns the hand a little toward quarte, as before.	Steps forward with the disengagement and lunges as before, then returns to guard and immediately steps backward.
Turns the hand a little toward sixte, as before.	Steps forward with the disengagement and lunges as before, returns to guard and immediately steps backward.

Parries and Ripostes

When taking quarte, the guard aids the forte in deflecting the attacker's blade. Quarte, like septime, exposes the extended target to potential attack. Septime is useful for defence against leg and foot attacks.

The counter-parry of sixte is useful in both foil and épée. Start by just relaxing the hand, so that the blade drops. The parry should be taken late. Next, rotate the hand so that it is horizontal, with the palm upward (supination). This puts the defender's blade directly on top of the attacker's blade. The attacker is now extremely vulnerable. Riposte may be covered or detached. A detached riposte is likely to be more effective with a late parry, since the opponent's point is more prone to pass the target.

Start at a distance where you can lay the tip of the blade on the opponent's guard.

Fencer A	**Fencer B**
1 In the on-guard position. Lays the tip of the blade on the (top) inside of the opponent's guard.	In the on-guard position. Practises circular actions using the fingers, with a little extra supination at the end to get on top of the opponent's blade.

Try to get this action as small as possible.

Fencer A	**Fencer B**
2 In the on-guard position. Lays the tip of the blade on the (top) inside of the opponent's guard.	In the on-guard position. Parries as before, but this time moves the hand 150mm forward at the same time.

This action, combined with a late parry, brings the point perilously close to the attacker's target.

Fencer A	**Fencer B**
3 In the on-guard position. Lays the tip of the blade on the (top) inside of the opponent's guard.	In the on-guard position. Parries as before, moving the hand forward, lifts the hand and drops the point at the same time.

Now the defender is well placed for a hit to arm, either direct, or indirect if Fencer A reacts toward sixte.

Indirect ripostes at épée can also be used effectively when the attacker's blade has passed the defender's body and the defender ripostes (with a bent arm) to body.

For the next exercise start at épée fencing measure.

Fencer A	**Fencer B**
1 In the on-guard position. Steps forward and backward arbitrarily, changing speed.	In the on-guard position. Keeps distance by stepping backward or forward with large or small steps (sometimes responding immediately, or after a slight pause), changing speed as necessary.
Launches attacks (occasionally) into the sixte and quarte lines.	Parries sixte or quarte and ripostes to arm or body (depending on distance), with or without a lunge as required.

2 In the on-guard position. Steps forward and backward arbitrarily, changing speed.	In the on-guard position. Keeps distance as before.
Launches attacks as before, then applies opposing pressure to the blade.	Parries sixte or quarte and disengages with the riposte.
3 In the on-guard position. Steps forward and backward arbitrarily, changing speed.	In the on-guard position. Keeps distance as before.
Launches attacks as before, withdrawing afterwards.	Parries sixte or quarte and ripostes to arm with a short lunge.
Parries sixte or quarte and starts to riposte	Does a simple parry on the lunge and counter-ripostes with opposition to the arm or body.

In the next exercise, Fencer A can stay on the lunge, or return to guard if Fencer B is to lunge with the riposte. The parries may be executed either early or late.

4 In the on-guard position. Steps forward and backward arbitrarily, changing speed.	In the on-guard position. Keeps distance as before.
	Parries sixte or quarte and
Launches a straight thrust, disengagement, beat attack or beat disengagement (if the opponent reacts).	ripostes to various parts of the target, with or without a lunge as required.

Next, Fencer B parries only deep attacks and ripostes, and does not react to feints or beats that are not followed by an attack, or attacks that are short. False attacks are not intended to hit, but to cause a reaction.

5 In the on-guard position. Steps forward and backward arbitrarily, changing speed.	In the on-guard position. Keeps distance as before.
Does a feint or beat, without finishing the attack, getting as	Reacts only to the deep attack, by parrying and riposting.

A parry of quarte.

close as possible using distance.
Occasionally does a deep
attack.

6	In the on-guard position. Steps forward and backward arbitrarily, changing speed.	In the on-guard position. Keeps distance as before.

Occasionally does short false
attacks, sometimes followed by
a sudden redoublement by
extending the length of the
lunge, or does a deep attack.

Reacts only to the redoublement or to the deep attack, by
parrying and riposting with
opposition.
• With the deep attack, it is
  essential to hold on to the
  blade.

A parry of raised sixte (sometimes called 'neuvieme'), is a supinated parry, useful in defending the upper target area. Start in sixte and simply lift the hand, turning the point inward a little.

Start at lunge distance for a hit to body.

Fencer A

Fencer B

1	In the on-guard position. Steps forward, straightening the sword arm with the hand held high.	In the on-guard position. Practises the parry of raised sixte and ripostes to the body. • Ensure that the opponent's point clears the mask.

2   In the on-guard position. Steps forward, straightening the sword arm with the hand held high.

In the on-guard position. Parries raised sixte, ducks down and ripostes to the knee.

3   In the on-guard position. Gives agreed signal for the training sequence to begin.

Takes a small step backward to avoid being hit.

After a pause, steps forward with the arm straight.

In the on-guard position. Lunges to hand/forearm.

Stays on the lunge with the sword arm straight.

Parries raised sixte (with the hand well forward) and ripostes as appropriate.

Improvising a high parry.

Counter-Ripostes

Start at épée fencing measure and gradually build up this sequence.

	Fencer A	**Fencer B**
1	In the on-guard position. Gives agreed signal for the training sequence to begin.	In the on-guard position. Steps forward quickly, straightening sword arm decisively with the landing of the rear foot. Lunges with a hit to body.
2	In the on-guard position. Gives agreed signal for the training sequence to begin. Parries late and ripostes to body.	In the on-guard position. Steps forward, straightens the sword arm and lunges as before.

	Fencer A	**Fencer B**
3	In the on-guard position. Gives agreed signal for the training sequence to begin.	In the on-guard position. Steps forward, straightens the sword arm and lunges to upper target of the body (short). • The fencers are at full lunge distance for a hit to body.
	Parries quarte.	Returns backward to guard. • The fencers are once again at lunge distance for a hit to body.
	Ripostes with a lunge to body.	Parries quarte and counter-ripostes to shoulder.

Or:

4	In the on-guard position. Gives agreed signal for the training sequence to begin.	In the on-guard position. Steps forward, straightens the sword arm and lunges to upper target of the body (short).
	Parries quarte.	Returns backward to guard. • The fencers are once again at lunge distance for a hit to body.
	Ripostes with a lunge to leg.	Parries septime and counter-ripostes to leg.
5	In the on-guard position. Gives agreed signal for the training sequence to begin.	In the on-guard position. Steps forward, straightens the sword arm and lunges to lower target.
	Parries seconde.	Returns to guard. • The fencers are at lunge distance for a hit to body.
	Ripostes with a lunge to hip/upper leg.	Parries octave and begins to counter-riposte to leg.
	Lifts the hand and attempts a redouble to the (top of) the arm.	Parries sixte and ripostes with opposition to the upper arm (explosively).

Practise counter-ripostes to various forward targets, with detached or covered ripostes. Counter-ripostes can be made successfully on the lunge, after a recovery and when advancing or retreating. As part of a more advanced training programme, additional counter-ripostes can be introduced by the defender.

A wide parry of octave.

Compound Attacks

The attacker must respond to the speed of the defender's actions. Varying the speed of different parts of a compound attack can create surprise. From the defender's point of view, a delayed parry can be harder to deceive.

Start at épée fencing measure. Fencer A will practise doing successful parries and ripostes.

Fencer A	**Fencer B**
1 In the on-guard position. Gives agreed signal for the training sequence to begin.	In the on-guard position. Attacks (briskly) with or without a step and lunge to various parts of the target area.
Takes an appropriate parry (with or without a small step backward), as late as possible. Ripostes to selected parts of upper and lower target areas, adjusting distance as required.	Recovers and steps backward (as required) to resume the correct distance.

Now the conditions are right for Fencer B to do a compound attack. The compound attack starts slow, accelerates, then finishes fast.

2	In the on-guard position. Gives agreed signal for the training sequence to begin. Takes an appropriate parry, as before.	In the on-guard position. Does a feint of attack with a step forward and starts to lunge. Deceives the late parry and finishes with a hit to an appropriate part of the target.

Next, Fencer A randomly varies early and late parries, with occasional counter-attacks. The use of delayed parries can mask the possibility that a counter-attack is imminent.

If a fencer shows a predominant interest in the upper lines of engagement, try feinting high and dropping low to leg or foot.

Start at épée fencing measure.

Fencer A	**Fencer B**
In the on-guard position. Gives agreed signal for the training sequence to begin. Steps backward. • The fencers are now at lunge distance for a hit to foot. • Fencer A is concentrating on defending the upper target.	In the on-guard position. Steps forward, feints an attack to upper target. Drops the point and lunges to foot (while opponent is temporarily distracted).

Dealing with Compound Attacks

Start at épée fencing measure. Fencer B comes on guard with the blade in octave.

Successive parries:

Fencer A	Fencer B
1 In the on-guard position. Steps forward and feints to the upper target area. • The fencers are now at lunge distance for a hit to body.	In octave. Attempts to parry with a semi-circular parry of sixte.
Deceives the blade.	Steps backward. • The fencers are once again at lunge distance for a hit to hand/forearm.
Does a small step forward following the disengagement. • The fencers are now at lunge distance for a hit to body.	Parries counter-sixte and ripostes with opposition to the upper arm.
2 In the on-guard position. Steps forward and feints to the upper target area. • The fencers are now at lunge distance for a hit to body.	In octave. Attempts to parry with a semi-circular parry of sixte.
Deceives the blade.	Steps backward. • The fencers are once again at lunge distance for a hit to hand/forearm.
Does a small step forward following the disengagement. • The fencers are now at lunge distance for a hit to body.	Parries quarte and ripostes with opposition to the upper arm.
3 In the on-guard position. Steps forward and feints to the upper target area. • The fencers are now at lunge distance for a hit to body.	In octave. Parries quarte, the hand moving diagonally from octave to quarte, cutting the line.
Deceives the blade.	Steps backward. • The fencers are once again at lunge distance for a hit to hand/forearm.

| Does a small step forward following the disengagement. | Parries counter-quarte and ripostes with opposition to the upper arm. |

• The fencers are now at lunge distance for a hit to body.

A time thrust can be used against the last action of a compound attack, if it is executed into a known line.

Start at épée fencing measure.

Fencer A	**Fencer B**
1 In the on-guard position. Disengages, feints to arm and starts to lunge.	In the on-guard position. Starts to parry quarte.
Disengages during the course of the lunge and attempts to hit to arm.	Immediately straightens the sword arm with a time thrust through sixte and hits to upper arm.
2 In the on-guard position. Disengages, feints to arm and starts to lunge.	In the on-guard position. Starts to parry quarte.
Disengages during the course of the lunge and attempts to hit to arm.	Immediately straightens the sword arm with a time thrust through counter-quarte and hits to upper arm.

Now perform the routine against a high–low attack. Fencer A starts with blade in octave at épée fencing measure.

Fencer A	**Fencer B**
1 In octave. Straightens the sword arm, feints to arm and starts to lunge.	In the on-guard position. Parries counter-sixte.
Counter-disengages during the course of the lunge and lowers the point for a hit to leg.	Parries octave or seconde and ripostes with opposition.

A double hit:

2	In octave. Straightens the sword arm and feints to the upper arm and starts to lunge.	In the on-guard position. Parries counter-sixte. Stop-hits to upper arm. Both hits land.
	Counter-disengages during the course of the lunge and lowers the point for a hit to leg.	

Then:

3	In octave. Straightens the sword arm, feints to the upper arm and starts to lunge.	In the on-guard position. Parries counter-sixte.
	Counter-disengages during the course of the lunge and lowers the point for a hit to leg.	Feints a stop-hit to arm.
	Attempts to parry sixte on the lunge.	Disengages and hits to arm.

Attacks on the Blade

A pressure can be applied that displaces the blade a little to the side. This can be followed by a direct attack with opposition, or as the defender reacts to the pressure, the attacker may finish in another line. The point moves faster than the legs and the attacker's hand should not remain still. When attacking the body, the guard may be used to deflect counter-attacks.

Start at épée fencing measure.

	Fencer A	**Fencer B**
1	In the on-guard position. Gives agreed signal for the training sequence to begin.	In the on-guard position. Takes a small step forward, applies a pressure (on either side of the centre of the blade) with the landing of the rear foot and does a short lunge to upper arm.

2 In the on-guard position. Gives agreed signal for the training sequence to begin.	In the on-guard position. Takes a small step forward and applies a light pressure, then suddenly applies hard pressure and does a short lunge to upper arm.

This sequence from an attack on the blade includes some other épée actions:

3 In the on-guard position. Gives agreed signal for the training sequence to begin.	In the on-guard position. Takes a small step forward and applies a light pressure, then suddenly applies hard pressure and starts to lunge with a feint to upper arm.
Reacts with a simple parry in the high line and takes a small step backward.	Drops the point to evade the high line parry and finishes the lunge with a hit to leg. Stays on the lunge.
Begins to move the hand forward.	Does a redoublement to the underside of hand/forearm on return to guard.
Lunges to arm.	Parries counter-sixte and steps in with angulated riposte to body, holding on to the blade. • Make sure that you do not get too close to the opponent and only hit lightly.

Beat attacks can be performed at different distances. Against a retreating opponent, an attack launched to upper arm can revert to lower positions down the arm or hand if the defender suddenly retreats. Against an advancing opponent, the beat attack into this advance will invariably revert to body. A beat attack to arm (which may be parried), can be followed by an immediate redoublement to body (sometimes with a flèche). The beat in épée tends to be harder than at foil. This is achieved by adding a little hand/forearm to the finger action and using the edge of the blade.

Start at épée fencing measure.

Fencer A	**Fencer B**
1 In the on-guard position. Gives agreed signal for the training sequence to begin.	In the on-guard position. Steps forward, executes a beat (on either side of the blade) as the rear foot lands, then begins to lunge with a deep attack.
Steps backward. The length of the step varies.	The hit lands with the completion of the lunge and is made on various parts of the hand/forearm, depending on the size of Fencer A's step.
2 In the on-guard position. Gives agreed signal for the training sequence to begin.	In the on-guard position. Steps forward, executes a beat as before, then begins to lunge.
Steps backward and attempts to parry.	Completes and stays on the lunge. Recovers to guard, forward. The back foot moves forward from the lunge position.
Takes a small step backward.	Disengages and flèches with a redoublement to body.
3 In the on-guard position. Steps forward, as if preparing to attack. • The fencers are now at lunge distance for a hit to body.	In the on-guard position. Executes a beat attack and lunges to body.
4 In the on-guard position. Carries out a series of deep attacks, using steps and lunges.	In the on-guard position. Retreats from deep attacks, keeping distance, occasionally launching a sudden beat attack into the opponent's preparation.

Another approach at épée fencing measure:

Fencer A	**Fencer B**
In the on-guard position. Gives agreed signal for the training sequence to begin.	In the on-guard position. Steps forward, executes a light false beat as rear foot lands. • The fencers are now at lunge distance for a hit to body.
No reaction.	Suddenly does a second hard beat.
Steps backward, reacting. • The fencers are now at lunge distance for a hit to hand/forearm or leg.	Lunges with hit to arm or leg.

A change beat occurs on the other side of the blade.
Start at épée fencing measure.

	Fencer A	**Fencer B**
1	In the on-guard position. Gives agreed signal for the training sequence to begin.	In the on-guard position. Takes a small step forward, lightly engages the blade in sixte, disengages around the blade and beats, with the hand speeding up, on the opposite side of the blade. Immediately straightens the sword arm and lunges with a hit to top shoulder.

If Fencer A steps backward, the hit can revert to hand/forearm. If a parry is added to the step backward, the hit can revert to toe, following a feint to top shoulder.

Prise de Fer Actions

The classical bind is one of the more useful prise de fer actions. Typically, the blade is taken on one of two upper engagements and ends up in a lower engagement, finishing on the lower body or upper leg. What follows are a sixte–septime bind and a quarte–octave bind.
Start at épée fencing measure, Fencer A moving backward and forward arbitrarily, with Fencer B responding.

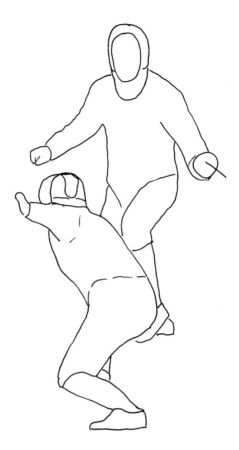

An attack to the foot.

Fencer A

1 In the on-guard position.
Straightens the sword arm occasionally.

2 In the on-guard position.
Straightens the sword arm occasionally.

Fencer B

In the on-guard position.
Steps forward, gathers the
blade in sixte and binds to septime.
Finishes with a hit to lower
body/leg.
• Be careful to adjust distance
  to suit.

In the on-guard position.
Steps forward, gathers the
blade in quarte and binds to
octave.
Finishes with a hit to lower
body/leg.

An épée fencer might deliberately go for a double hit, if there is a marginal lead in the score, evading the prise de fer.

Fencer A	Fencer B
In the on-guard position. Gives agreed signal for the training sequence to begin.	In the on-guard position. Steps forward and attempts to engage the blade using a counter-sixte action and lunges to body.
Counter-disengages, evading the blade, and straightens the sword arm, creating a double hit.	

Actions against Prises de Fer

Against an attempted prise de fer one can execute a ceding parry or an opposition parry, or one can deceive the attempted taking of the blade.
    Start at épée fencing measure.

	Fencer A	Fencer B
1	In the on-guard position. Steps forward and gathers the blade through counter-sixte and starts to lunge to body. • The fencers are at lunge distance for a hit to body. • Fencer A is attempting to dominate the top of the opponent's blade and may supinate the hand a little in order to achieve this.	Starts with the sword arm straight. Cedes to prime and ripostes to body. • In prime, the point is also well placed for a hit to leg.
2		Starts with the sword arm straight.
	In the on-guard position. Steps forward and gathers the blade through counter-sixte and starts to lunge to body.	Opposes with a parry of sixte and ripostes with opposition to body/top shoulder.

- The fencers are at lunge
  distance for a hit to body.

(Left-handed/right-handed combination: with 1. and 2., Fencer B cedes to sixte or opposes to quarte.)

Having mastered these training exercises, additional footwork and choices of target can be added.

Next, try to ensure that the dérobement is as small as possible. Get the point out immediately. Start at épée fencing measure.

Fencer A	**Fencer B**
1	Starts with the sword arm straight.
In the on-guard position. Steps forward and attempts to gathers the blade through counter-sixte.	Immediately does a dérobement and hit to arm as the opponent steps forward.

In the next example, Fencer A attempts to draw the dérobement in order to launch a beat attack.

2	Starts with the sword arm straight.
In the on-guard position. Steps forward and attempts to gather the blade through counter-sixte. • The fencers are now at lunge distance for a hit to body.	Immediately does a dérobement and straightens the sword arm.
Launches beat attack on blade and starts to lunge to body.	Immediately stop-hits to the arm off the beat and steps backward. • The fencers are now at step and lunge distance for a hit to body.
Finishes the lunge, short.	Parries quarte with the hand well forward and ripostes to the arm with opposition.

(Left-handed/right-handed combination: Fencer B may need to parry sixte and riposte to the arm with opposition.)

Counter-Attacks

Whilst stop-hits can be directed to any part of the body, a stop-hit to the opponent's torso will often result in a double hit. Stop-hits may be practised to the body, upper arm, forearm and finally to the hand (with increasing difficulty).

A counter-attack into the opponent's preparation.

Stop-hits can be executed above or below the hand. Hits below the hand are best carried out with the hand in pronation, sometimes with a slight bend of the knees. The choice of where to place the point will depend on the position of the attacker's hand. For example, against a high hand the counter-attacker may go underneath, or against a low hand on top. Hitting the extended target requires considerable skill. As you may sometimes miss, the stop-hit can be followed by a parry and riposte.

Start at épée fencing measure.

Fencer A	**Fencer B**
1 In the on-guard position. Steps forward and straightens the sword arm with hand at shoulder height. • The fencers are now at lunge distance for a hit to body. Completes the lunge (short).	In the on-guard position. Counter-attacks below the hand/forearm and steps backward. • Fencer B has successfully counter-attacked into the opponent's preparation.
2 In the on-guard position. Steps forward and straightens the sword arm with hand at shoulder height. • The fencers are now at lunge distance for a hit to body.	In the on-guard position. Counter-attacks below the hand/forearm, immediately parries quarte and ripostes with opposition. • The parry and riposte with opposition ensure that Fencer B's hit does not land.
3 In the on-guard position. Steps forward and straightens the sword arm, lowering the hand a little for a hit to leg. Completes the lunge (short).	In the on-guard position. Counter-attacks to top of hand/forearm and steps backward. • Fencer B has successfully counter-attacked into the opponent's preparation.
4 In the on-guard position. Steps forward and straightens the sword arm, lowering the hand a little for a hit to leg.	In the on-guard position. Counter-attacks to top of hand/forearm, immediately parries seconde or octave and ripostes with opposition. • The parry and riposte with opposition ensure that Fencer B's hit does not land.
5 In the on-guard position. Steps forward and straightens the sword arm, lowering the hand a little for a hit to leg.	In the on-guard position. Counter-attacks to top of arm.

| Attempts to lunge to leg. | Withdraws the front foot, moving from the on-guard position and bringing the heels together in a standing position.
• Moving the foot back ensures that the leg is out of distance.
• Fencer B's hit has priority. |

This action of withdrawing the front foot to avoid the attacker's point is called a rassemblement. This is a classic épée stroke, in which the counter-attacker finishes in a standing position with the arm and blade elegantly bearing down on to the attacker's forearm (like casting with a fishing rod). In some cases, the front foot may only need to withdraw a little. The role of the rear arm is crucial in ensuring that balance is maintained.

A rassemblement.

Next, a stop-hit with a disengagement:

| **6** In the on-guard position. Steps forward and attempts to take the blade with an engagement, or a change of engagement.
• The fencers are now at lunge distance for a hit to body.

Completes the lunge (short). | In the on-guard position. Disengages and counter-attacks to hand/forearm and steps backward.

• Fencer B has successfully counter-attacked into the opponent's preparation. |

A compound stop-hit:

7	In the on-guard position. Steps forward and attempts to take the blade with an engagement, or a change of engagement. • The fencers are now at lunge distance for a hit to body.	In the on-guard position. Feints a counter-attack.
	Parries as necessary.	Disengages and hits to hand/forearm. • Fencer B has successfully counter-attacked into the opponent's preparation.

A stop-hit with a duck-down:

8	In the on-guard position. Steps forward and straightens the sword arm, attempting to hit the hand/forearm.	In the on-guard position. Ducks down to avoid being hit and stop-hits to the underside of the hand/forearm.

To duck down, bend the knees, being sure to keep your weight evenly distributed between your feet, and extend the arm with the hand above your head to deflect the attacker's blade. Do not touch the piste with your unarmed hand.

A stop-hit may not always be successful, so it can be followed with a remise or a redoublement.

9	In the on-guard position. Steps forward and straightens the sword arm with hand at shoulder height. • The fencers are now at lunge distance for a hit to body.	In the on-guard position. Counter-attacks below hand/forearm.
	Lowers the hand, blocking the counter-attack with the guard, then lifts the hand.	Remises below the hand/forearm and steps backward.
10	In the on-guard position. Steps forward and straightens the sword arm with hand at shoulder height.	In the on-guard position. Feints a counter-attack to the hand/forearm.

- The fencers are now at lunge distance for a hit to body.

Attempts to parry.	Disengages and attempts to hit the hand/forearm.
Parries again, this time successfully.	Disengages and does a redoublement to the hand/forearm.

Counter-attacks can be executed with opposition, starting at épée fencing measure. The time thrusts that follow are executed in a single movement which intersects the opponent's final (known) line.

Start at épée fencing measure.

Fencer A	**Fencer B**
1 In the on-guard position.	In octave.
Straightens the sword arm and steps forward, starting to lunge.	Suddenly rotates the hand through counter-octave, taking the blade and straightening the sword arm with a hit to body. • This is done all in one action.

This version avoids a double hit.

Fencer A	**Fencer B**
2 In the on-guard position.	In octave.
Straightens the sword arm and steps forward, starting to lunge.	Rotates the hand through counter-octave, attempting to take the blade.
Does a counter-disengagement during the course of the lunge and attempts to hit to body.	Side-steps to avoid the opponent's point. • Only Fencer B's hit lands.
3 In the on-guard position.	In octave.
Straightens the arm and steps forward.	Rotates the hand through counter-octave, attempting to take the blade.
Does a counter-disengagement.	Stop-hits to the forearm then steps backward.

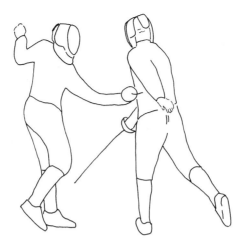

Moving to one side to avoid the opponent's point.

| Lunges short | • Only Fencer B's hit lands. |

Actions against Counter-Attacks

Draw the opponent's stop-hit during a training routine. Start at épée fencing measure. The fencers start by moving backward and forward slowly, taking great care not to get too close.

Fencer A	**Fencer B**
1 In the on-guard position. Gives agreed signal for the training sequence to begin.	In the on-guard position. Does false attacks with short steps forward, stepping backward occasionally.
Keeps distance. Occasionally straightens the sword arm.	Practises prises de fer when the timing and distance are suitable and the opponent's sword arm is straight. • Both fencers must be careful not to get too close.

Next:

| **2** In the on-guard position. Gives agreed signal for the training sequence to begin. | In the on-guard position. Does false attacks as before. |

Keeps distance. When ready, launches counter-offensive actions, with or without a disengagement.	Either continues the attack with lunge and opposition, or parries and ripostes. Both fencers must be careful not to get too close.
3 In the on-guard position. Gives agreed signal for the training sequence to begin.	In the on-guard position. Does false attacks as before.
Keeps distance. When ready, launches counter-offensive actions, with or without a disengagement.	Steps backward to avoid being hit, occasionally launches a beat attack (with footwork to suit), to arm or body. • Both fencers must be careful not to get too close.

Renewed Offence and Counter-Offence

The persistent attacker/counter-attacker is likely to renew. A short attack/counter-attack can be used to draw a parry and riposte from an opponent. An alternative to counter-riposting is to remise on to the extended target ahead of the riposte.

If an opponent has a strong parry, but hesitates or sometimes makes no riposte, then a redoublement can be used. This can be done as a deliberate act of second intention, or as a learned response.

A reprise (combined with a redoublement) can be executed by recovering forward or backward. In a typical reprise forward at épée, the rear foot moves only three-quarters of the way forward, ensuring that the redoublement is immediate. In the less common reverse reprise, the recovery is made by moving backward to the on-guard position, the front touching the floor briefly, after which a new lunge is launched immediately.

At épée fencing measure. Start with a remise.

Fencer A	**Fencer B**
1 In the on-guard position. Moves the hand a little toward quarte.	In the on-guard position. Lunges to hand/forearm.
Parries sixte.	Stays on the lunge.

Releases the blade.
- The hand moves a little forward.

The point lands on the forearm as the opponent's hand moves forward.
- The remise.

Add a redoublement.

2 In the on-guard position.
Moves the hand a little toward quarte.

In the on-guard position.
Lunges to hand/forearm.

Parries sixte.

Stays on the lunge.

Releases the blade.
The hand moves a little forward.

The point lands on the forearm as the opponent's hand moves forward.
- The remise.

Moves the hand a little toward sixte.

Disengages and hits to arm, extending the lunge a little.
- The redoublement.

Add a reverse reprise with a redoublement.

3 In the on-guard position.
Moves the hand a little toward quarte.

In the on-guard position.
Lunges to hand/forearm.

Parries sixte.

Stays on the lunge.

Releases the blade.
The hand moves a little forward.

Point lands on the forearm as opponent's hand moves forward.
- The remise.

Moves the hand a little toward sixte.

Disengages and hits to arm, extending the lunge a little.
- The redoublement.

Moves the guard a little toward quarte.

Recovers backward with the arm still straight, the front foot briefly touching the ground. Disengages and lunges immediately with hit to arm, without pausing.

• A reverse reprise with a redoublement.

Actions against Renewals

To stop a remise landing on the arm, hold on to the blade when you riposte, or lift the hand, displacing the extended target away from the attacker's point riposting (immediately) with angulation to your opponent's arm. To stop a redoublement landing, do a second parry and hold on to the blade when you riposte.

Fencing at Close Quarters

Corps à corps exists when two fencers are in contact. At foil and sabre, it is forbidden for a fencer to cause corps à corps. At all three weapons, it is forbidden for a fencer to cause corps à corps intentionally to avoid being hit, or to jostle an opponent. At épée, a fencer who brings about corps à corps (without brutality or violence), for example by touching guards, has not committed a fault. Use of the unarmed hand and turning your back on an opponent is forbidden. If the blades can no longer be manipulated, then the referee will call 'halt'. If the blades can still be manipulated, then close quarters fencing is allowed.

Closing distance may occur through an unsuccessful flèche attack, or

Suddenly at close quarters.

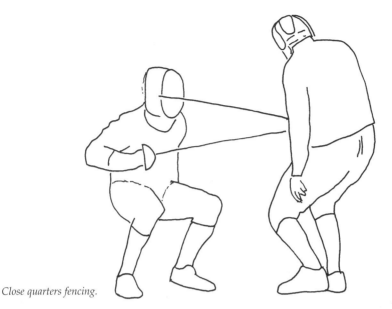

Close quarters fencing.

perhaps by stepping in to avoid a riposte landing after the opponent has taken the blade. The position that both fencers find themselves in will often not have been pre-planned. The fencer who steps backward from this position will quite often be hit, because this merely exposes the target. Instead, if you can move sufficiently close to your opponent to demonstrate that the blades can be no longer manipulated, then the referee will call 'halt'.

Hits at close quarters tend to be delivered with a bent arm and with angulation, delivered to leg or body. Parries (or engagements of the blade) in the high line should be made with the hand lower and in the low line with the hand higher, with the blade more vertical. Close quarters fencing at foil is similar, although the hits are directed to the trunk of the body and the back is particularly vulnerable if the opponent ducks down.

To practise, fencers should stand close together, turn inward a little and at times even get alongside the opponent. Concentrate on placing the hit slowly using thumb and forefinger. Remember that the épée has a stiff blade and light hitting is essential.

Fencer A	**Fencer B**
1 Engaged in sixte. Gives agreed signal for the training sequence to begin.	Engaged in sixte. Applies pressure to the outside (centre) of the opponent's blade. Places the point (lightly) on the opponent's chest, with the arm still bent and holding on to the blade.

Practise three hits in succession.

	Fencer A	Fencer B
2	Engaged in sixte. Gives agreed signal for the training sequence to begin.	Engaged in sixte. Applies pressure as before, places the point on the opponent's chest, places a second hit 50mm over (toward opponent's quarte side), then a third hit a further 50mm over (in the same direction).
3	Engaged in sixte. Gives agreed signal for the training sequence to begin.	Engaged in sixte. Turns hand from sixte to tierce with (sudden) turn of the wrist (holding on to opponent's blade), ripostes (lightly) with opposition to chest.

(Left-handed/right-handed combination: the opponent's blade is on Fencer B's outside. Fencer B is covered.)

Then practise with a close-quarters engagement in prime.

	Fencer A	**Fencer B**
1	In the on-guard position. Gives agreed signal for the training sequence to begin.	Starts with the hand (held high) in prime and the opponent's blade engaged, lowers the hand (still holding on to the blade) and places the point (lightly) on to the leg

Start at lunge distance for a hit to body.

2	In the on-guard position. Gives agreed signal for the training sequence to begin.	In the on-guard position. Steps inside, passing the opponent's point and approaching close quarters, lifts the hand into prime with no engagement. Finishes with a hit to upper leg.

Lastly, at épée fencing measure.

3   In the on-guard position. Steps in gradually, concluding at close quarters.

In the on-guard position. Parries counter-sixte (late) holding on to blade as the opponent approaches close quarters. Ripostes with opposition to chest, keeping the sword arm bent.

A riposte with opposition.

CHAPTER NINE

Coaching Épée

A Few Thoughts

Tactical training for épée requires energy and agility. The coach who wishes to coach all day long will need to conserve energy, keeping all motion to the minimum, while ensuring that the student gets a good workout. The coach will be mobile, lunging, stepping forward and backward, stop-hitting, remising, parrying and riposting, and so on. Point accuracy is important, particularly in relation to the arm and leg target areas. Always stress point first, then feet. Coaching is done with absence of blade. Training may be done using a hard or soft (leather) training sleeve. The soft version is the easier of the two to hit consistently, enabling a quicker build-up of confidence.

The following lesson/training session is good for developing co-ordinated arm and foot movements. With modification, this can be performed with any weapon (remember to leave out the crossover forward and the flèche if doing sabre). At foils and sabre the engagement might be done using quarte. As usual, the coach takes the part of Fencer A.

Start at épée fencing measure. We shall explore some blade preparations, with a variety of footwork. Practise each routine sequentially until you can do the whole session from beginning to end without stopping, then vary the timing.

Fencer A	Fencer B
1 In the on-guard position. Gives agreed signal for the training sequence to begin.	In the on-guard position. (In your own time.) Steps forward and engages the blade (as the rear foot lands) with a counter-sixte action, straightens the sword arm (holding on to blade) and hits to arm, all without pausing, then steps backward. • The fencers are once again on guard at épée fencing measure.

2 In the on-guard position.

In the on-guard position.
(In your own time.)
Steps forward, moving the feet close together (the heels touch) and engages the blade with a counter-sixte action, straightens the sword arm as before.
Returns to guard at épée fencing measure.

3 In the on-guard position.

In the on-guard position.
(In your own time.)
Steps forward and engages the blade with a counter-sixte action and starts to straighten the sword arm (holding on to blade).

Steps backward.
• The fencers are once again at épée fencing measure

Lunges and hits to hand/forearm then returns to guard.
As before, the action is continuous.

4 In the on-guard position.

In the on-guard position.
(In your own time.)
Steps forward, moving the feet close together (the heels touch) and engages the blade with a counter-sixte action and starts to straighten the sword arm.

Steps backward.

Lunges and hits to upper arm.
Returns to guard at épée fencing measure.

With the second action, the defender is under much greater pressure and the hit lands further up the arm.

5 In the on-guard position.

Counter-disengages and straightens the sword arm (attacking into slow preparation).

In the on-guard position.
(In your own time.)
Steps forward and attempts to engage the blade with a counter- sixte action.

• It important that the blades do not touch.	Parries quarte with hand well forward, immediately ripostes to the arm with opposition. Returns to guard at épée fencing measure.

The purpose of the parry in this training sequence is to pave the way for the beat that will be attempted next.

6 In the on-guard position. Counter-disengages and straightens the sword arm.	In the on-guard position. (In your own time.) Steps forward and attempts to engage the blade with a counter-sixte action. • The fencers are now at lunge distance for a hit to body. Immediately does a beat attack and lunges to body. Returns to guard at épée fencing measure.

The next exercise is a repeat of 3., but we will develop it a little further.

7 In the on-guard position.	In the on-guard position. (In your own time.) Steps forward and engages the blade with a counter-sixte action and starts to straighten the sword arm (holding on to blade).
Steps backward. • The fencers are once again at épée fencing measure	Lunges and hits to hand/forearm, then returns to guard.
8 In the on-guard position.	In the on-guard position. (In your own time.) Steps forward slowly and engages the blade lightly with a counter-sixte action.
Steps backward. • The fencers are once again at épée fencing measure.	Steps forward quickly, firmly holding on to the engagement (applying extra pressure).

Steps backward, responding immediately to the sudden change of pace. • The fencers are once again at épée fencing measure	Lunges fast with a hit to hand/forearm, then returns to guard.
9 In the on-guard position.	In the on-guard position. (In your own time.) Steps forward slowly and engages the blade lightly with a counter- sixte action.
Steps backward. • The fencers are once again at épée fencing measure.	Steps forward quickly, moving the feet close together (the heels touch), firmly holding on to the engagement.
Steps backward, responding immediately to the sudden change of pace.	Lunges fast with a hit to upper arm. Returns to guard at épée fencing measure.
10 In the on-guard position.	In the on-guard position. (In your own time.) Steps forward and engages the blade with a counter-sixte action.
Steps backward twice.	Does crossover (one leg moves over the other) and lunges to an appropriate part of the target. Returns to guard at épée fencing measure.
11 In the on-guard position.	In the on-guard position. (In your own time.) Steps forward and engages the blade with a counter-sixte action. • The fencers are now at lunge distance for a hit to body.

Moves backward a little.
* The distance is now between lunge distance and a step and lunge distance to body.

Does a flèche attack to the body.
Returns to guard at épée fencing measure.

12   In the on-guard position.

In the on-guard position.
(In your own time.)
Steps forward and engages the blade with a counter-sixte action.
* The fencers are now at lunge distance for a hit to body.

Steps backward.
* The fencers are now at step and lunge distance for a hit to body.

Does a sudden balestra (a jump forward followed by a lunge) with a hit to body.
* The balestra initiates a sudden change of pace, taking the opponent by surprise.
Returns to guard at épée fencing measure.

13   In the on-guard position.
Steps forward.

In the on-guard position.
Moves the rear foot backward only, does a beat and hits with a lunge to arm.
Returns to guard at épée fencing measure.

14   In the on-guard position.
Steps forward.

In the on-guard position.
Moves the front foot forward only, does beat and hits with a lunge to upper arm.
Returns to guard at épée fencing measure.

Glossary

Absence of blade not crossing swords with the opponent's blade.
Advance a movement forward by step, crossover or balestra.
Advanced target the arm, at sabre and épée.
Angulation to angle the blade with pronation or supination.
Appel a blow on the ground made with the ball of the foot as a preparation.
Attack an attempt by the fencer to hit the opponent.
Attack au fer an attack that is prepared by deflecting the opponent's blade.
Balestra a jump forward followed by some more footwork.
Beat a striking action on the opponent's blade, used as a preparation.
Bind when the blades are engaged, carrying the opponent's blade diagonally across from high to low line or low to high line.
Bout one individual fight.
Broken time when two or more movements are made, deliberately causing a sudden change in tempo, which fools the opponent into responding at the wrong time.
Cadence the rhythm in which a sequence of moves is made.
Ceding parry a defence against prise de fer.
Change beat a beat executed with a change of engagement.
Change of engagement passing from one engagement to another, by moving under the blade.
Choice reaction reacting differently to a change of conditions presented by an opponent.
Close quarters when fencers are too close to use their weapons properly, but without body contact.
Compound attack an attack that comprises one or more feints.
Conventions the code of rules governing foil and sabre fencing.
Coquille the bell-shaped guard on a foil or épée.
Corps à corps when two fencers are in contact.
Coulé starts by gliding along the adverse blade, keeping it in opposition, raising the hand at the last minute to create a sudden opposition of forte to foible.
Counter-attack an offensive action into an offensive action, which gains a period of fencing time.
Counter-disengagement a disengagement in the opposite direction, to deceive a counter-parry.

Counter-parry another name for a circular parry.
Counter-riposte an offensive action following the successful parry of the riposte or counter-riposte.
Counter-time any action made by an attacker on the opponent's attempt to stop-hit or stop-cut.
Coupé another name for a cutover.
Covered riposte where the parrying blade stays in contact with the attacker's blade during the riposte.
Croisé carrying the opponent's blade from high to low line, or low to high line, on the same side as the engagement.
Crossover moving forward or backward by crossing one leg over the other.
Cut a hit with the cutting edge of the blade at sabre.
Cutover a form of disengagement that passes over the point of the opposing blade.
Cutting the line parrying by moving diagonally from one line to another.
Defence avoiding a hit, moving out of distance, or parrying.
Defensive box the area to be covered by the defender.
Dérobement the successful deception of an attack au fer, or prise de fer.
Detached riposte where the parrying blade releases contact with the attacker's blade during the riposte.
Direct a simple attack or riposte that finishes in the same line in which it was formed, with no feints out of that line.
Disengagement an indirect simple attack or riposte hitting in the opposite line, by passing under the opponent's blade.
Displacement moving the target to avoid being hit.
Double cutover a compound attack.
Double hit two hits that arrive together.
Engagement when the blades are in contact.
Envelopment where the weak part of the opposing blade is taken by the strong part of the attacker's blade, describing a circle, with both blades in contact, returning to the same line of engagement.
Extended target the sword arm target area at sabre and épée.
False attack an attack that is not intended to hit, but causes a reaction.
Feint in general, a blade movement meant to resemble an attack and whose purpose is to draw a reaction.
Fencing the art and science of handling the sword.
Fencing measure the distance at which one can hit the opponent's target with a lunge.
Fencing time the time required to perform one simple fencing action.
First defensive triangle prime, seconde, quinte.
Flank the side of the trunk of the body on the sword arm side.
Flèche in which the aggressor leaps off the leading foot, attempts to make the hit, then passes the opponent at a run.

Flying riposte the parry is taken with a backward hand action, followed by a cutover riposte.

Foible the upper weak part of the blade.

Forte the strong part of the blade nearest the guard.

Froissement displaces the opponent's blade by a strong grazing action.

Fundamental elements of fencing these are the use of timing speed and distance.

Guard the metal cup that protects the hand from being hit; also a defensive fencing position.

Grip the way in which the weapon is held.

Half-parry a parry taken (in sabre) with a forward hand position.

High–low attack a type of compound attack (at foil and épée).

Hit to strike the opponent with the point with the character of penetration, or a cut at sabre.

Indirect a simple attack or riposte that finishes in a different line to the one in which it was formed.

In line a position in which the sword arm is straight and the point of the weapon threatens the valid target.

Judges in non-electric fencing four judges can watch for hits.

Lunge an attack made by extending the rear leg and landing on the bent front leg.

Molinello a circular forward rotation of the hand and wrist, terminating with the point to target at foil and cut at sabre.

Neuvieme the ninth line of engagement.

Offensive–defensive position a position in sabre from which the fencer may attack or defend.

Offensive–defensive parry see half-parry.

On guard the ready position adopted before the word 'play'.

One–two attack a type of compound attack (at foil and épée).

'Open eye' training a method of training where a fencer selects responses to a coach's (or another fencer's) various actions, as though in a real fighting situation.

Opposition parry holding and resisting the blade during the parry.

Orthopaedic handle (or grip) a moulded handle (at foil and épée).

Parry a defensive action made with the blade to prevent the attack from landing.

Passé an attack that passes the target without hitting.

Phrase a set of related actions performed without a break.

Piste the linear strip on which a fencing bout is fought.

Pistol grip see orthopaedic handle.

Plastron a padded over-jacket worn while training or coaching; also the term used for a half-jacket with no underarm seam, worn for extra protection on the sword arm under the fencing jacket.

Point in line an extended arm and blade that threatens the opponent's target.

Pommel a metal counter-balance secured at the end of a French handle which locks the parts of the weapon in place.

Pommelling fencing holding the pommel of the foil or épée.

Preparation any movement that prepares the way for an attack.

Pressure pressing against the opponent's blade, in order to deflect it or get a reaction.

Principle of defence the opposition of forte against foible.

Prise de fer a taking of the blade.

Progressive attack an attack of more than one movement executed in one period of fencing time.

Pronation with the palm facing downwards, the opposite of supination.

Rassemblement moving from the on-guard position and bringing the heels together in a standing position.

Recovery return to the on-guard position, by moving forward or backward.

Redoublement a renewal of attack in a different line.

Referee the person who supervises safety in a bout and awards the hits.

Renewed offence see remise, reprise and redoublement.

Remise a renewal of attack in the same line.

Reprise a renewal of attack passing through the on-guard position (forward or backward).

Retreat to step or jump backward, the opposite of advance.

Right of way rules for awarding the point in the event of a double touch at foil and sabre.

Riposte the offensive action made by the fencer who has successfully parried the attack.

Second defensive triangle tierce, quarte, quinte.

Second intention a premeditated action used to draw a response from the opponent, which prepares the way for the intended action that follows.

Semicircular parry a deflection of the blade by making a semicircle (or 'U'-shaped gathering action) with the point.

Side-step see displacement.

Simple executed in one movement, an attack or riposte that involves no feints.

Simultaneous attacks two attacks (in foil and sabre), for which the right of way is too close to determine.

Stance the position of the feet and part of the on-guard position.

Step backward a backward movement made with both feet, rear foot first, moving one at a time without crossing.

Step forward a forward movement made with both feet, front foot first, moving one at a time without crossing.

Stop-cut a stop-hit with the edge of the blade, in sabre, typically to the wrist.

Stop-hit a counter-offensive action that lands before the attacker's final movement.

Straight thrust a direct attack landing in the same line.

Successive parries a response to a compound attack.

Supination with the palm facing upwards, the opposite of pronation.

Teaching position a stance that helps to reduce the coach's physical effort while training a fencer.

Through cut a circular cut made with the flat of the blade at sabre.

Time-hit a stop-hit with opposition.

Time thrust a single movement taken with opposition that intersects the opponent's final line.

Trompement a deception of the opponent's attempt to parry.

Valid hit a hit that arrives correctly on target.

A coach demonstrating to a class.

Bibliography

Books and brochures

Beke, Z, and Polgár J, *The Methodology of Sabre Fencing* (Corvina Press, Budapest, 1963)

Bracewell, H T, *Foil Personal Proficiency Course* (1987)

Crosnier, R, *Fencing with the Épée* (Faber and Faber Ltd, London, 1958)

Crosnier, R, *Fencing with the Foil* (Faber and Faber Ltd, London, 1967)

Crosnier, R, *Fencing with the Sabre* (Faber and Faber Ltd, London, 1954)

DeSilva, H, *Fencing: The Skills of the Game* (The Crowood Press Ltd, 1991)

Garret, M R, Kaidanov, E G and Pezza, G A, *Foil, Saber, and Épée Fencing* (The Pennsylvania State University Press, 1999)

Gaugler, W M, *A Dictionary of Universally Used Fencing Terminology* (Laureate Press, 1997)

Kingston, T, *Épée Combat Manual* (Terence Kingston, 2001)

Llewellyn, J, *County Training Group Programme, Épée* (British Fencing, 1989)

Lukovich, I, *Fencing* (Alföldi Printing House, Debrecen, 1986)

Pitman, B, *Fencing: Techniques of Foil, Épée and Sabre* (The Crowood Press Ltd, 1999)

Pitman, B, *Manual for the B A F Basic Foil, Épée and Sabre Coaching Awards*

Simmonds, A T and Morton E D, *Fencing to Win* (The Sportsman's Press, 1994)

Skipp, A, *Know the Game: Fencing* (A & C Black (Publishers) Ltd, 1994)

Szabó L, *Fencing and the Master* (SKA Swordplay Books, 1997)

Videos

Tyshler, D, *Épée Fencing – Parts 1 and 2,* Roussky Dom Co., Moscow

Websites

www.classicalfencing.com
www.fencing.ca
www.fencing.net
www.fencing.school

A training routine.

Ed Rogers (left) and Bert Bracewell (right).

Index

Absence of blade 13–17, 39, 47, 48, 55, 56, 57, 58, 60, 73, 74, 104, 162, 222
Advance 29, 60
Angulation 55, 65, 66, 68, 93, 160, 170, 218, 219
Appel 37
Attack 22, 42, 75, 139, 160, 175, 190
Attack au fer 69, 137, 144

Balestra 13–17, 37, 125, 137, 163
Beat 37, 64, 73, 74, 84, 119, 120, 137, 144, 146, 150, 194, 204, 224
Bind 37, 78, 184, 206
Bout 147
Broken time 89, 90, 158, 159

Cadence 227
Ceding parry 80, 177, 208
Change beat 37, 206
Change of engagement 37
Choice reaction 90, 98, 99, 137
Close quarters 43, 177, 218, 219, 220
Compound attack 32, 39, 60, 89, 114, 125, 128, 180, 199
Conventions 10, 102
Coquille 20, 179
Corps à corps 218
Coulé 37
Counter-attack 85, 122, 140, 142, 160, 168, 183, 185, 190, 210, 214
Counter-disengagement 22, 36, 42
Counter-parry 26, 29, 134, 178, 192

Counter-riposte 30, 53, 54, 55, 96, 113, 131, 134, 166, 197, 199, 216
Counter-time 123, 187
Coupé 22
Covered riposte 199
Croisé 37, 49, 78
Crossover 13–17, 22, 37, 125
Cut 107, 108, 163
Cutover 22, 26, 141, 175
Cutting the line 48

Defence 6
Defensive box 104
Dérobement 82, 85, 146
Detached riposte 27
Direct 53, 108, 111, 132, 175, 177, 193
Disengagement 22, 23, 33, 42, 86, 141, 176
Displacement 86
Double hit 168, 185, 203, 208, 214

Engagement 37, 120, 138, 146, 219, 220, 222
Envelopment 37, 184
Extended target 170, 177, 210, 216, 218

Feint 32, 114, 132, 180, 194
Fencing 6
Fencing measure 11, 104, 170
First defensive triangle 111
Flèche 13–17, 22, 87, 204, 222
Flying riposte 78, 79

Foible 26, 177
Forte 26, 177
Froissement 37
Fundamental elements of fencing
    6

Guard 13–17, 104, 168
Grip 20, 106, 171, 172

Half-parry 143
High-low attack 34, 39, 202
Hit 20

Indirect 22, 54, 108, 111, 112, 132,
    175, 177, 193
In line 144

Judges 103

Lunge 11, 104, 170, 173

Molinello 78

Neuvieme 19, 195

Offensive-defensive position 103
Offensive-defensive parry 143
On guard 12, 103, 170
One-two attack 32, 65
'Open eye' training 42
Opposition parry 80, 81, 177, 208
Orthopaedic handle (or grip) 19,
    171

Parry 26, 42, 44, 47, 110, 112, 127,

131, 144, 166, 177, 192, 194,
    210, 216, 219, 222
Passé 168
Piste 10
Pistol grip 19
Plastron 7, 10
Pommel 171
Pommelling 171, 172
Preparation 37, 39, 40, 69, 70, 71,
    119, 137, 165, 183, 222
Pressure 37, 203
Principle of defence 26, 177
Prise de fer 77, 144, 177, 183, 206
Progressive attack 32, 127
Pronation 27, 34, 54, 68

Rassemblement 212
Recovery 13, 170, 172
Redoublement 148, 188, 189, 204,
    213, 216, 217
Referee 10, 102, 103
Renewed offence 148, 188, 216
Remise 49, 108, 148, 160, 188, 190,
    212, 213, 216, 222
Reprise 13, 149, 188, 216, 217
Right of way 10, 26, 27
Riposte 27, 35, 42, 47, 49, 111, 117,
    132, 143, 160, 177, 182, 192,
    193, 194, 210, 216, 218, 222

Second defensive triangle 111
Second intention 48, 83, 134, 140,
    216
Semicircular parry 26, 29, 178
Side-step 86
Simple 22, 33, 42, 65, 78, 108, 113,
    119, 125, 132, 134, 140, 142,
    175, 190
Simultaneous attacks 147, 168
Step backward 13–17, 37, 35, 37,
    125, 127, 131, 137, 138, 140,
    170, 222

Step forward 13–17, 37, 119, 125, 137, 138, 170, 222
Stop-cut 122, 123, 131, 140, 141, 142, 144
Stop-hit 85, 123, 183, 185, 186, 210, 212, 213, 222
Straight thrust 22, 42
Successive parries 35, 66, 117, 182, 201

Supination 170, 172

Teaching position 94, 162
Through cut 107
Time-hit 185, 186
Time thrust 47, 88, 202, 214

Valid hit 10, 11, 102